Reading Strategies for Spanish Speakers

Susan Davis Lenski
Fabiola Ehlers-Zavala
Illinois State University

KENDALL/HUNT PUBLISHING COMPANY
4050 Westmark Drive   Dubuque, Iowa 52002

Book Team

Chairman and Chief Executive Officer   Mark C. Falb
Director of National Book Program   Paul B. Carty
Editorial Developmental Manager   Georgia Botsford
Assistant Vice President, Production Services   Christine E. O'Brien
Prepress Project Coordinator   Angela Shaffer
Prepress Editor   Ellen Kaune
Permission Editor   Renae Heacock
Cover Designer   Jodi Splinter

Books by Susan Davis Lenski

Improving Reading: Strategies and Resources (3rd ed.) (with Jerry L. Johns)
Improving Writing: Strategies, Assessments, Resources (2nd ed.) (with Jerry L. Johns)
Reading & Learning Strategies: Middle Grades through High School (with Mary Ann Wham and Jerry L. Johns)
Early Literacy Assessments and Teaching Strategies (with Jerry L. Johns and Laurie Elish-Piper)
Comprehension and Vocabulary Strategies for the Primary Grades (with Jerry L. Johns and Roberta Berglund)
Becoming a Teacher of Reading: A Developmental Approach (with Susan L. Nierstheimer)

Author Information for Correspondence and Workshops

Susan Davis Lenski
Illinois State University
Campus Box 5330
Normal, IL 61790-5330
sjlensk@ilstu.edu
(309) 438-3028

Fabiola Ehlers-Zavala
Illinois State University
Campus Box 5330
Normal, IL 61790-5330
fabponce@ilstu.edu
(309) 438-8860

Ordering Information

Address: Kendall/Hunt Publishing Company
4050 Westmark Drive
Dubuque, IA 52002

Telephone: 800-247-3458, Ext. 5

Website: www.kendallhunt.com

Contents

Preface

WHO WILL USE THIS BOOK?

Reading Strategies for Spanish Speakers was written for monolingual and bilingual teachers of Spanish-speaking students who are learning to read English. Some of these teachers will also be teaching students to read in their heritage language, Spanish, and this book is also for them.

WHAT ARE SOME OF THE UNIQUE CHARACTERISTICS OF THIS BOOK?

This book was patterned after the successful Kendall/Hunt Reading Resources such as *Improving Reading: Strategies and Resources* and *Reading & Learning Strategies: Middle Grades through High School.* The authors of *Reading Strategies for Spanish Speakers* selected 27 strategies that they thought would help Spanish-speaking students learn to read English and/or Spanish. The strategies are contextualized with evidenced-based research and theory and are clearly written with step-by-step directions and examples. Some of the unique characteristics of this book are the following:

- ◆ Examples in English and Spanish—to assist teachers who teach reading in both English and Spanish,

- ◆ Reproducibles of strategies in English and Spanish—to provide maximum flexibility in instruction for bilingual teachers,

- ◆ Examples of children's literature from Latin America—to help students identify with texts being read,

- ◆ Variations—to provide teachers with ideas for adapting the strategies,

- ◆ Assessment Ideas—for teachers to use to determine how well students are learning, and

- ◆ Websites—for teachers to use for additional resources.

WHAT GRADE LEVELS DO THE STRATEGIES ADDRESS?

The strategies in this book can be used for students as young as kindergarten and as old as high school.

Preface

HOW TO USE THIS BOOK

You can use *Reading Strategies for Spanish Speakers* in a number of ways. To begin, you should look at the Quick Reference Guide on the inside front cover to determine your Instructional Goals. The Quick Reference Guide lists the Instructional Goals covered in each chapter of the book. Note that the chapters are divided into Prereading Strategies, During Reading Strategies, and After Reading Strategies. Decide which kinds of reading strategies you want to teach and refer to the Instructional Goals for more specific information.

Chapter 2 ❧ Prereading Strategies

SECTION 2.1 To promote the development of background knowledge and to encourage students to access the knowledge that pertains to texts being read 16

SECTION 2.2 To help students become familiar with word meanings before reading so they can comprehend texts 31

SECTION 2.3 To teach students how to use text structure to increase comprehension 46

TESOL STANDARDS

Another way to approach the teaching of reading to Spanish speakers is to cross-reference the strategies you teach with the TESOL Standards. To do this, you would look at the chart on pages 10 and 11. Look at the Standard you want to reinforce and then choose one of the strategies that applies to the Standard. For example, if you wanted to emphasize TESOL Goal 1, Standard 3, you can choose from several different strategies that help students meet that standard.

FIGURE 2. *English as a Second Language (ESL) Standards for PreK–12 Students*

	TESOL STANDARD	CHAPTER 2									CHAPTER 3									CHAPTER 4								
		1	2	3	4	5	6	7	8	9	10	11	12	13	14	15	16	17	18	19	20	21	22	23	24	25	26	27
G	**Standard 1** To use English to communicate in social settings: Students will use English to participate in social interactions	■	■	■	■	■	■	■	■	■	■	■	■	■	■	■	■	■	■	■	■	■	■	■	■	■		■
O **A**	**Standard 2** To use English to communicate in social settings: Students will interact in, through, and with spoken and written English for personal expression and enjoyment			■	■											■	■	■					■	■				
L **I**	**Standard 3** To use English to communicate in social settings: Students will use learning strategies to extend their communicative competence				■	■	■				■	■	■	■	■	■								■			■	■

ENGLISH AND SPANISH REPRODUCIBLES

If you are teaching students who are proficient in English but have a Spanish-language background, you may want to teach the strategies in this book using the English reproducible with the suggested children's literature. If your students are more comfortable learning strategies in Spanish, however, you can use the Spanish reproducible and teach the specific strategy using a copy of a

Spanish children's book and the Spanish reproducible. The Spanish reproducibles have been translated into Spanish so that you can teach students in the language with which they learn best. At times, you might consider teaching a strategy to your entire class and have students work independently in their dominant language.

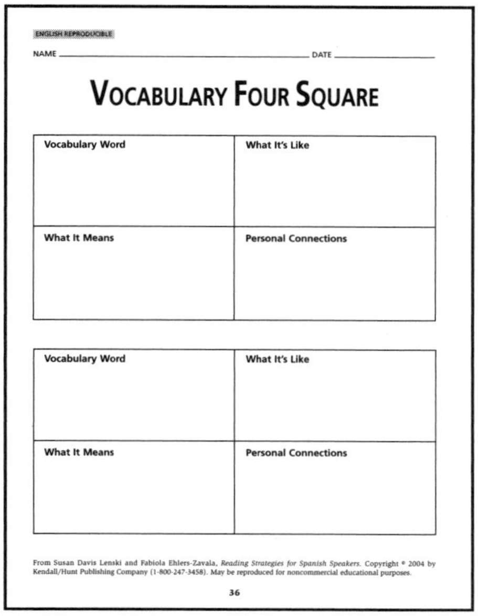

ENGLISH REPRODUCIBLE	SPANISH REPRODUCIBLE
NAME _____ DATE _____	NOMBRE _____ FECHA _____
VOCABULARY FOUR SQUARE	**VOCABULARY FOUR SQUARE**

English reproducible (page 36):

Vocabulary Word	What It's Like
What It Means	Personal Connections

Vocabulary Word	What It's Like
What It Means	Personal Connections

From Susan Davis Lenski and Fabiola Ehlers-Zavala, *Reading Strategies for Spanish Speakers*. Copyright © 2004 by Kendall/Hunt Publishing Company (1-800-247-3458). May be reproduced for noncommercial educational purposes.
36

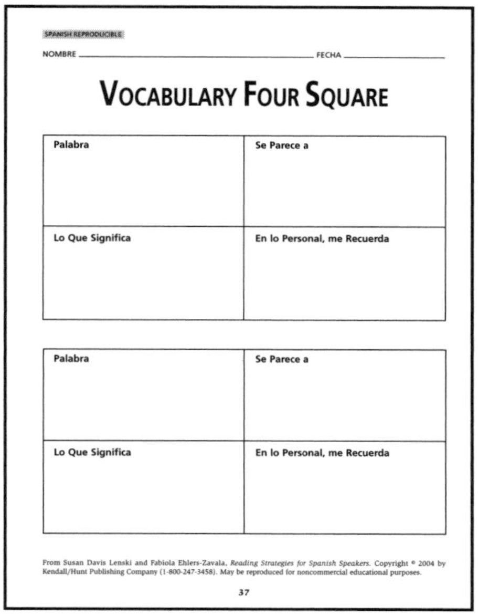

Spanish reproducible (page 37):

Palabra	Se Parece a
Lo Que Significa	En lo Personal, me Recuerda

Palabra	Se Parece a
Lo Que Significa	En lo Personal, me Recuerda

From Susan Davis Lenski and Fabiola Ehlers-Zavala, *Reading Strategies for Spanish Speakers*. Copyright © 2004 by Kendall/Hunt Publishing Company (1-800-247-3458). May be reproduced for noncommercial educational purposes.
37

VARIATIONS

Good teachers adapt strategies to different teaching situations. We've given you some ideas under the feature titled "Variation" to provide suggestions for ways to use the strategy in new ways. You'll find ideas for Variations sprinkled throughout the book. Feel free to adapt these strategies in other ways as well.

VARIATION

You can change the labels on the four quadrants based on the age of your students and their language proficiency. Students just learning a second language are often helped if you include an illustration. The illustration can be presented next to the word. The illustration often helps students cement their knowledge of the word's meaning. To meet the needs of learners who are more advanced in their language development/acquisition process, you may consider it more challenging to provide an antonym for the given term in the box for *Personal Connections*. For instance, for students who are gaining proficiency in English or students who are native English speakers, you should consider changing the label *Personal Connections* to *Opposites*. In this quadrant students should write examples of words or phrases that are different from the vocabulary word. When students think of ideas that are opposite to the word they are learning, they enlarge their conceptual understanding of that word.

ASSESSMENT IDEAS

Teachers of Spanish speakers continually assess their students both formally and informally. In the feature titled "Assessment Idea" we've given you some ways to use the reading strategy to assess students' reading. As you use these strategies, you'll think of additional ways to assess students that you can use to inform your teaching.

ASSESSMENT IDEA

The Vocabulary Four Square can also be used as an assessment tool. When students are familiar with a word's meaning, you can give them the Vocabulary Four Square reproducible to assess their conceptual knowledge of the word. This type of assessment is much more comprehensive than merely asking students to give a definition for a word.

WEB RESOURCES

Helpful websites have been distributed throughout the book to give you additional resources about teaching Spanish-speakers to read. Some of the websites are links to professional organizations and others provide teaching ideas. Remember, though, that web addresses change without warning so some of the websites might not be available for use when you try to access them.

 = **Directions and Examples**

 = **Group Activities**

 = **Reproducible Student Worksheets**

 = **Web Resources**

Acknowledgments

We truly appreciate the cheerful, willing help we received as we wrote this book. Among those of our friends, students, colleagues, and teachers who gave us encouragement and ideas, we'd like to specially thank the following people:

◆ Maria Aguirre and Mariana Alvayero for their thoughtful feedback and help with translations,

◆ Eve Dinardi for assistance with typing,

◆ Denise Holmes for photography,

◆ Fran Lenski for copyediting, and

◆ Brigham Elementary School students for pictures and inspiration.

About the Authors

Susan Davis Lenski is a Professor at Illinois State University, in the Department of Curriculum and Instruction, where she teaches undergraduate and graduate courses in reading, writing, and language arts and is the Director of the Center for Reading & Literacy. Dr. Lenski brings 20 years of experience as a public school teacher to her work as a professor. As a result of her practical experience and her grounding in theory, Dr. Lenski is a popular speaker for professional development programs and has consulted in the United States, Canada, Panama, and Guatemala.

Susan Lenski has been recognized for her work by a variety of organizations. For her work as a teacher, she received the *Nila Banton Smith Award* and an *Exemplary Reading Program Award*, both from the International Reading Association. Dr. Lenski was inducted into the Illinois Reading Hall of Fame in 1999, and was named Outstanding Researcher for the College of Education at Illinois State University. Susan Lenski has co-authored 11 books, including *Improving Reading: Strategies and Resources* (with Jerry L. Johns), and has published over 65 articles in state and national journals. Her research interests include incorporating reading and writing strategies into classroom practice, content area reading, and preparing culturally responsive teachers.

Fabiola Ehlers-Zavala is an Assistant Professor of Bilingual Education at Illinois State University where she teaches undergraduate and graduate courses in the theoretical foundations of bilingual education as well as methods and materials, assessment, and program design and implementation. A native of Chile, Dr. Ehlers-Zavala brings a realistic view of learning English to her work with English-language learners (ELLs) in addition to more than 10 years of experience teaching English as a second language. She is a strong supporter of development and maintenance of ELLs' heritage languages.

Fabiola Ehlers-Zavala's primary areas of research are second language reading and quality bilingual/ESL/EFL teacher preparation. She has disseminated her research through numerous presentations delivered at the annual meetings of TESOL (Teachers of English to Speakers of Other

Languages), NABE (National Association for Bilingual Education), AAAL (American Association for Applied Linguistics), and ITBE (Illinois TESOL/ Bilingual Ed.). Some of her articles have appeared in TESOL Journal, Mex TESOL, and Revista Chilena de Estudios Norteamericanos. The Illinois Association of Supervision and Curriculum Development has recognized Dr. Ehlers-Zavala's research on second language reading with an honorary mention of the Winn Research Award. Fabiola Ehlers-Zavala has been active in professional organizations, and she is currently ITBE President.

Teaching Reading to Spanish Speakers

1

he ability to read in a first or second language is important for students' personal, academic, and future professional success. For this reason, teachers in all academic contexts and teaching scenarios are greatly concerned with the challenge of providing their students with strategies to maximize their potential as effective readers. Indeed, regardless of an area of expertise or a domain for which a teacher has been trained, attention to literacy development cannot be brushed aside in the hope that a reading support teacher can compensate for what all teachers should systematically and continually embrace across levels, subject areas, and program types: the effective development of all readers.

In light of current demographic changes showing that Hispanic learners are having an increasingly significant presence in United States schools, *Reading Strategies for Spanish Speakers* was written to provide teachers of English and Spanish speakers with a repertoire of reading strategies that could be implemented in a variety of teaching contexts. These teaching contexts could range from classrooms in which English is the only medium of instruction to classrooms that are bilingual. The strategies were selected to appeal to learners whose native language is Spanish. Since the strategies chosen were selected for their universal appeal, however, teachers can apply them in contexts characterized by rich or varied linguistic diversity.

CLASSROOM COMPOSITION, AIMS, AND CHALLENGES

Critical to the implementation of a sound curriculum that focuses on the development of reading skills of all learners is the clear understanding of the teaching context. This is true for teachers who are trained to work with linguistically and culturally diverse learners (i.e., bilingual and/or ESL teachers) as well as general education teachers who may or may not have received the necessary training to effectively meet the needs of these learners.

The challenges that many teachers in general education classrooms currently face cannot be underestimated because, in many instances, they are confronting demands for which they may not have been trained. For instance, general education teachers may find themselves assisting learners who may be native speakers of English but who may speak a nonstandard variety of English (e.g., Black English Vernacular). Teachers may also find themselves assisting learners who are not native speakers of English. This situation may very well entail having teachers assist learners who are in the process of developing a language other than English as their native language and who still may be far from acquiring English as their second language.

The challenges that bilingual instructors face in regard to the teaching of reading are likely to be doubled. When teaching in weak forms of bilingual education, that is, programs that aim at transitioning students into English-only classrooms (i.e., transitional bilingual education/early exit programs), teachers are constantly battling against time. There is simply not enough time to provide English-language learners with strong support to develop reading skills to tackle academic material in either their first (e.g., Spanish) or second language (e.g., English).

Additionally, when teaching in strong forms of bilingual programs, that is, programs that aim at helping learners become fully bilingual (e.g., dual language programs), the task of a bilingual teacher is compounded by the exigencies of helping learners develop skills to process texts in two languages. After all, the word "bilingual" implies the development of two languages on the part of a speaker. Depending on the language combination, the task may be either facilitated or complicated even further due to the nature of the linguistic systems to be addressed. Facilitation may be experienced when the two systems allow for the positive transfer of skills learned in one language onto the other. Difficulty may emerge when transfer is not positive and interference, instead, occurs (Birch, 2002).

Furthermore, these complexities can be elevated to another level. This is so by virtue of knowing that there can be different kinds of bilingualism. That is, there seem to be different routes to bilingualism (Baker, 2001), and this would have an impact on the resources bilinguals have available to perform various cognitive tasks, as is the case of comprehending any given written text. Some people become bilingual by virtue of acquiring one language first and then the other. This is typically observed among bilinguals who learn their second language in a foreign language environment (e.g., a Chilean learner who speaks Spanish as a first language and takes English as a foreign language at school). Others become bilingual by virtue of being immersed in a context where two languages are in regular contact, as is the case of families who speak two languages in the United States/Mexican border communities.

Many classrooms have English-language learners in them.

Consequently, to a considerable extent, the nature of the educational program in which teachers operate will either narrow or expand the strategic choices any teacher may have available to help learners become effective readers. Further, the teachers' prior pedagogical experiences and certification are likely to mediate the choices of strategies that can or cannot be effectively implemented in their classrooms. Last but not least, the nature of the learners will add to the set of questions a teacher must consider prior to final decision making regarding the strategies to implement for effective reading instruction.

CLASSROOM CONTEXTS

Soltero (2004) has developed a chart that can help teachers understand the multiplicity of educational programs beyond general education programs for mainstream learners that exist in the United States educational system to meet the needs of linguistically and culturally diverse learners. (See Figure 1.) This is a sample of main programmatic educational alternatives; it is not an exhaustive list of all the possible program options. Teachers can refer to the chart to decide the appropriateness of teaching reading strategies in English or in Spanish in light of the educational goals of each particular program type.

FIGURE 1. *Educational Models for Second-Language Learners in the United States*				
Language/s	**Names**	**Population**	**Linguistic Outcome**	**Curriculum and Number of Years**
Native Language and English	*Immersion* Dual language Two-way immersion Enrichment Two-way bilingual	English-language learners (who speak the same language) and native English speakers	*Additive* Bilingualism and biliteracy in L1 and English	Content in L1/L2 Long term (6–12 years)
	Maintenance Development Enrichment Heritage language	English-language learners (who speak the same language)	*Additive* Bilingualism and biliteracy in L1 and English	Content in L1/L2, ESL Long term (6–12 years)
	Traditional Early-exit	English-language learners (who speak the same language)	*Subtractive* Monolingualism in English	Content in L1, rapid transition to L2, ESL Short term (1–3 years)
	Transitional Late-exit	English-language learners (who speak the same language)	*Subtractive* Monolingualism in English	Content in L1 with transition to L2, ESL Long term (4–6 years)
English	*Structured English Immersion*	English-language learners (who speak the same language or speak different languages)	*Subtractive* Monolingualism in English	ESL, sometimes limited L1 support Short term (1–3 years)
	ESL	English-language learners (who speak the same language or speak different languages)	*Subtractive* Monolingualism in English	Pull-out or in class Short term (1–3 years)
	Newcomer Centers	English-language learners (who speak the same language or speak different languages)	*Subtractive* Monolingualism in English	ESL, Sheltered English Short term (1–2 years)
	Submersion	English-language learners (who speak the same language or speak different languages) placed in mainstream English classrooms	*Subtractive* Monolingualism in English	No ESL or L1 support

From Soltero, S. W. (2004) *Dual language: Teaching and learning in two languages.* Boston: Allyn and Bacon. Reprinted with permission.

KEY CONSIDERATIONS

Programmatic decisions related to the education of English-language learners are often times restricted by the characteristics of situational contexts in which those decisions are made (e.g., state mandates, financial and human resources, number of speakers of any given language). Thus, many teachers have limited possibilities for pedagogical choices. Regardless of the program choice, one thing is clear: English-language learners are expected to learn to read in English, and teachers are expected to do whatever it takes to help learners achieve this goal. Because of the challenges this task may entail, teachers are also expected to make instructional adjustments to meet the needs of all learners. In doing so, teachers will benefit from the task of providing learners with a repertoire of reading strategies that learners can use to tackle different reading experiences. After all, "good readers use many strategies and techniques to help themselves understand print texts of various types" (Grongnet, Jameson, Franco, & Derrick-Mescua, 2000, p. 28).

Learning to read in English challenges not only the learners themselves but also their respective teachers. English-language learners typically are far from constituting a homogeneous group; therefore, they can range from students who are emergent literacy learners in their first language to those who are proficient readers. Literacy in the first language mediates literacy in the second language. Thus, literacy experiences students may have had in their first language will influence their ability, for better or worse, to perform in literacy activities in the second language. The spectrum of abilities and levels of reading proficiency may be quite vast in any classroom. While it is virtually impossible to predict the nature of the learners any given teacher may have, what we can do is to bring to teachers' attention a few considerations to keep in mind about their prospective students:

◆ English-language learners by definition are speakers of other languages, other linguistic systems. Accordingly, they have acquired (in varying degrees and aspects, consciously or unconsciously) the rules (morphological, syntactical, phonological, semantic, and pragmatic) that govern the linguistic systems they identify as their native languages. This means that English-language learners have internalized certain rules that govern their native languages and are likely to use them to understand and acquire other linguistic systems.

◆ English-language learners also, by definition, are in the process of learning English, a linguistic system that involves *other* sets of governing rules that may or may not be similar to the English-language learners' native language. For this reason, a conscious attempt on the part of the teacher (regular education or bilingual) must be made to help learners acquire English integrated with content instruction. The language development of English-language learners cannot be left to be addressed by English as a second language (ESL) teachers or bilingual educators only. Regular education teachers must actively seek the formal preparation needed (i.e., ESL and/or bilingual course work) to help meet the needs of English-language learners.

◆ For English-language learners, acquiring English is very challenging, particularly if their point of comparison at any given grade level is their native English peers. Native English speakers always represent, for English-language learners, "a moving target." That is, "while ELLs are developing their English, native English speakers continue to increase their vocabularies and develop even more sophisticated language skills" (Grongnet, Jameson, Franco, & Derrick-Mescua, 2000, p. 51). That is why they inevitably represent a moving target for English-language learners.

◆ English-language learners, as is the case of native speakers of English, have diverse educational experiences, both classroom and nonclassroom based. Teachers cannot assume that their students have the needed strategic competence to succeed in various reading tasks.

It is more likely that English-language learners will become proficient readers if they apply the reading strategies that good readers use. Too often, however, teachers of English-language learners spend the bulk of their time helping students with translation and other tasks rather than teaching students to apply the types of strategies students need to think deeply and comprehend texts. The purpose of this book is to provide teachers with a tool to use to teach English-language learners, and English only students as well, with the types of strategies that promote proficient comprehension of text.

STRATEGIC INSTRUCTION

In order for the teaching of reading strategies to be effective with English-language learners, it is important for teachers, as they prepare to plan instruction for English-language learners, to accomplish four basic tasks.

1. Teachers should formally and informally assess prior experiences students may have had in regard to literacy (ranging from concepts about print, prior experience in regard to text types and topics, to family literacy practices).
2. Teachers should formally introduce the various strategies they choose to implement, using a variety of reading materials/topics.
3. Teachers should model the use of the strategies in diverse reading contexts so that students observe how the strategies can be applied in different learning situations.
4. Teachers should provide ample opportunities and appropriate pacing for students to use the strategies in the classroom independently and as part of collaborative and cooperative practices with their peers.

Further, as teachers implement the instruction of reading strategies, it is important that they do so by providing a balanced interactive approach to reading development. English-language learners, as do their peers who are native speakers of English, need plenty of practice not only with text-driven strategies that involve bottom-up approaches to reading instruction (e.g., automatic word recognition and syntactical forms) but also with reader-driven strategies that emphasize higher-order thinking skills (e.g., ability to formu-

Teachers should make reading accessible to students through strategic instruction.

late predictions, infer information) as is the case of top-down approaches to reading. Only when these strategies are situated and approached from an interactive perspective to reading development will instructors begin to see their students succeed in becoming effective readers.

INSTRUCTIONAL ACCOMMODATIONS

Depending on the students' language competencies, teachers may need to make instructional accommodations to make the presentation or use of reading strategies comprehensible to learners. Teachers should model the use of the strategies and provide learners with ample learning opportunities to apply these reading strategies in a variety of reading materials. The accommodations that students need are grounded on principles of sheltered instruction (Echevarria & Graves, 2003), and they revolve around the following premises:

◆ Modifying instruction to meet the needs of learners;

◆ Providing hands-on activities to maximize student involvement, both independent and collaborative;

◆ Bringing realia into the classroom;

◆ Responding to various learning styles by providing learning experiences that are rich in a variety of visual, auditory, tactile, and olfactory experiences; using technology (ranging from the use of an overhead projector to the use of sophisticated multimedia when available);

◆ Demonstrating the use of strategies to learners and their parents or custodians to promote school-home connections for enhanced literacy experiences;

◆ Maintaining high expectations while providing appropriate scaffolding to empower all learners; and

◆ Attending to affective factors that may influence reading development, such as being sensitive to students' own multicultural heritages.

ABOUT THIS BOOK

Reading Strategies for Spanish Speakers was written for teachers of Spanish-speaking students who are learning English. Depending on the classroom context, students may also be learning to read and write in their heritage language, Spanish. *Reading Strategies for Spanish Speakers* could also be used for dual language classrooms in which English-speaking students are learning to read and write in Spanish. The selection of reading strategies presented in this book was made to ensure a reasonable degree of flexibility on the part of teachers who wish to implement them in their classrooms. The strategies can be used in either entirely monolingual or entirely bilingual contexts. Thus strategies are presented in two languages (English and Spanish). Keep in mind, however, that the decision to choose between the English version of a strategy or the Spanish version must be made by considering the program models in which teachers are working and in accordance with the desires of the students' parents or caregivers (see the International Reading Association's position on second-language learning, 2001).

This book does not intend to advocate for one educational program or another, for such is a decision that must be made at the local level, involving all its stakeholders in the education of native and nonnative speakers of English. Instead, this book is intended as a resource that will provide its readers with a selection of strategies that can be used with native and nonnative speakers of English to promote their successful mastery of reading skills in English, and whenever possible in Spanish as well. Consequently, the strategies in this book are provided in both English and Spanish for two main reasons. First, this bilingual version facilitates the task of general education teachers who may be able to provide Spanish support services to their learners in their classrooms and promote the healthy development of Spanish as their native or heritage language. When this is the case, if the general education teacher is not bilingual, it is advisable to have, at the very least, a properly trained and certified bilingual paraprofessional who can provide additional support and feedback to the learners in the use of the strategy. If Spanish support systems are not available (e.g., trained paraprofessionals, translators), the teacher then is encouraged to use the strategy in English with the appropriate accommodations to ensure successful mastery of the strategy on the part of the learners.

Finally, it is important to note that these strategies were chosen because they are helpful to promote reading comprehension in many languages. This statement, however, does not intend to suggest that languages are identical. Different languages do represent different linguistic systems with different conventions. Teaching reading in bilingual programs should not be approached in entirely identical ways. "Teaching children to read in Spanish is NOT the same as teaching children to read in English" (Escamilla, 2000, p. 125). This means that initiating beginning learners into reading should not necessarily be approached in identical ways. Nevertheless, the strategies presented here work with many linguistically and culturally diverse learners at various stages of the reading process (i.e., before, during, and after reading), thus helping readers reach the goal of becoming effective readers.

ENGLISH AS A SECOND LANGUAGE (ESL) STANDARDS

The professional organization TESOL (Teachers of English to Speakers of Other Languages) developed standards to provide a guideline for instruction for English-language learners, not just Spanish speakers but speakers of all languages who are learning English (TESOL, 1997). (See Figure 2.) These standards are known as the national English as a Second Language (ESL) Standards for PreK–12 Students. The standards have three main goals with three standards within each goal. The goals of the ESL standards are for students:

♦ to use English to communicate in social settings,

♦ to use English to achieve academically in all content areas, and

♦ to use English in socially and culturally appropriate ways.

Although our view in this book is to encourage biliteracy in English and Spanish, and we have provided strategies that have been translated into both languages, we acknowledge the importance of students learning to communicate in English in North America. Therefore, we have also aligned the strategies that we have selected for this book with the ESL standards with the understanding that one of the priorities of all teachers will be for their students to become proficient speakers, readers, and writers of English.

We recommend that teachers select strategies from each of the chapters so that students are learning how to become strategic readers throughout the reading process (before, during, and after reading). We also encourage teachers to select strategies to teach that represent each of the ESL standards. When using guidelines for teaching students to be strategic readers and by teaching strategies that are covered by the ESL standards, teachers can have the best chance of teaching the strategies that all students need to become effective readers.

Teachers of English to Speakers of Other Languages
www.tesol.org
Website for professional orgranization. Gives standards, references, information about conferences, and advice for teachers of English to speakers of other languges.

International Reading Association
www.reading.org
Website for professional orgranization in reading. Contains materials and ideas for teachers of reading.

National Association for Bilingual Education
www.nabe.org
NABE is a professional organization that tracks federal policy related to bilingual education, offers publications including a journal (available for order from the website), provides discussion forums, and sponsors an annual conference, for which you can register online.

Center for Applied Linguistics
www.cal.org
CAL is a professional organization dealing with linguistic issues.

FIGURE 2. *English as a Second Language (ESL) Standards for PreK–12 Students*

TESOL STANDARD	CHAPTER 2								
	1	2	3	4	5	6	7	8	9
GOAL 1 *Standard 1* To use English to communicate in social settings: Students will use English to participate in social interactions	■	■	■	■	■	■	■	■	■
Standard 2 To use English to communicate in social settings: Students will interact in, through, and with spoken and written English for personal expression and enjoyment			■	■					
Standard 3 To use English to communicate in social settings: Students will use learning strategies to extend their communicative competence				■	■	■			■
GOAL 2 *Standard 1* To use English to achieve academically in all content areas: Students will use English to interact in the classroom	■	■	■	■	■	■	■		■
Standard 2 To use English to achieve academically in all content areas: Students will use English to obtain, process, construct, and provide subject matter information in spoken and written form	■	■	■	■	■	■	■		■
Standard 3 To use English to achieve academically in all content areas: Students will use appropriate learning strategies to construct and apply academic knowledge	■	■	■	■	■	■	■	■	■
GOAL 3 *Standard 1* To use English in socially and culturally appropriate ways: Students will use the appropriate language variety, register, and genre according to audience, purpose, and setting					■	■	■		
Standard 2 To use English in socially and culturally appropriate ways: Students will use nonverbal communication appropriate to audience, purpose, and setting									
Standard 3 To use English in socially and culturally appropriate ways: Students will use appropriate learning strategies to extend their sociolinguistic and sociocultural competence									

CHAPTER 3									CHAPTER 4								
10	11	12	13	14	15	16	17	18	19	20	21	22	23	24	25	26	27
■	■	■	■	■	■	■	■	■	■	■	■	■	■	■	■		■
					■	■	■					■	■				
■	■	■	■	■								■			■		■
	■		■	■	■	■	■	■	■	■	■	■					■
	■	■		■	■	■	■	■	■	■	■	■	■	■	■	■	■
■	■	■	■	■	■	■	■	■	■	■	■	■	■	■	■	■	■

Prereading Strategies

eading is a complex, interactive process that involves a reader, a text, and a context. This process is made more complex when the person learning to read is also developing proficiency in a new language. Brisk and Harrington (2000) state that students learning to read in a new language need "to know the language, especially the written form of the language; they need to know literacy; and they need to have prior knowledge of the topic. They also need to put all this knowledge together when reading and writing" (2000, p. 7). Students who are learning to read and also learning the language, therefore, are developing two difficult cognitive processes simultaneously.

In order to know how to read, Ediger (2001) suggests that students need skills and knowledge in the following areas:

- ◆ Automatic recognition skills—the skills to recognize text in the new language,

- ◆ Vocabulary and structural knowledge—the knowledge of word meanings and the language structure,

- ◆ Formal discourse structure knowledge—the knowledge of the way texts are organized in the new language,

- ◆ Content/world background knowledge—text-related knowledge and an understanding of cultural implications,

- ◆ Synthesis and evaluation skills/strategies—the ability to think critically and decide how to use information, and

- ◆ Metacognitive knowledge and skills monitoring—an awareness of one's understanding and mental processes.

These areas of instruction can guide teachers as they prepare lessons for students learning to read. Many teachers find that dividing reading instruction into three areas—prereading, during reading, and after reading—can facilitate students' learning.

The use of prereading strategies is the most important part of instruction for teachers of English-language learners (ELLs). During prereading, teachers can help students become interested in the text by building their familiarity with the topic. One of the most difficult aspects of reading in a new language is the lack of understanding of cultural implications in texts. Teachers can overcome this barrier by helping students access the background knowledge that they have and in helping students build background knowledge when necessary. As teachers prepare prereading lessons, therefore, they need to be aware of their students' understandings and interests so they can design activities that engage students with the ideas in the texts.

Even students who are interested in a topic will have difficulty reading if they do not know the meanings of the words in the selection. Teachers of ELLs need to spend time preparing students for reading by teaching vocabulary words. Teaching vocabulary should be approached in two ways. First, students who are learning English (or Spanish) need to be able to read words in their lexicons, or their personal store of words. These words often do not need further vocabulary instruction because the students know the meaning of the words. For example, if students were reading the story *Uncle Nacho's Hat*

(Rohmer, 1989) they might know the meanings of the words "mercado," "visita," and "basura" in Spanish but not know the words in English. These students simply need to learn the English equivalents in order to read the book. For students who do not know the meaning of the word "baúl," however, they need to learn not only the English word for "trunk" but also what the word means. As teachers develop prereading strategies for vocabulary building, therefore, they need to teach students not only the words in the new language but also the meanings of new vocabulary words.

Teachers who are developing prereading lessons should also consider teaching students how texts are organized. Teachers in North America are typically very competent in teaching students that fictional texts have characters, setting, plot, and theme, but when teachings ELLs, they need to make these story devices more visible. Students who are learning English may have had experiences listening to Spanish stories and/or reading books in Spanish. Martínez-Roldán (2003) suggests that Spanish-speaking students are influenced by their background experiences hearing narratives told in Spanish which tend to be less linear than English stories. As teachers work with ELLs, therefore, they need to be aware that English and Spanish stories may indeed have organizational differences and students learning English may need to have explicit instruction in the ways texts are organized in English.

Pablo is learning English words in preparation for reading a new book.

Prereading strategies can help prepare students for reading a text, especially if teachers think of the skills and strategies students need to be able to read with comprehension. Students are far more likely to become successful readers if they have background knowledge about the topic, if they are able to read the words in the selection, and if they have an understanding of the way that the texts are organized. The strategies in this chapter can provide teachers with ideas for accomplishing these goals.

ESL Bears

www.eslbears.homestead.com

This is a multimedia learning designated for first-year immigrant students. It has any activities appropriate for students whose English ability ranges from entry level to intermediate.

SECTION 2.1 Developing and Accessing Background Knowledge

> *Instructional Goal:* **To promote the development of background knowledge and to encourage students to access the knowledge that pertains to texts being read**

BACKGROUND

Reading comprehension is dependent on knowledge of the topic of the text (Rummelhart, 1980). This knowledge is called "background knowledge." Background knowledge of the topic of a text helps readers assimilate new information into existing knowledge structures, making it possible for increased comprehension. For example, if you read an article about dieting, you will probably be able to read it quickly with a high degree of comprehension because you have knowledge about the topic. If you read something on an unfamiliar topic, though, you will probably need to apply a variety of reading strategies to comprehend the text.

We often hear teachers lament, "My students have no background knowledge." This simply isn't so: all students have background knowledge. What teachers really mean is that some students do not have prior knowledge about a topic of importance to the teacher, possibly a topic of a text that teachers want students to read. Teachers need to realize that students from cultures other than the mainstream school culture may know different things, have different values, and have different experiences than the teacher has (Dyson, 2003). This realization is powerful because it helps teachers recognize that their students do possess a great deal of background knowledge. Once teachers recognize that all students have background knowledge, they can move on to valuing each student's individual knowledge and experience.

Even though value judgments should not be placed on background knowledge, students who were raised speaking the English language have what Bourdieu and Passeron (1977) have termed "cultural capital." Cultural capital is the culturally valued advantages that students have as a result of their background and life experiences. Standard English, for example, is valued in North American schools, and students who have been raised listening to and speaking Standard English have the cultural capital of the language. Conversely, students who speak Spanish have cultural capital that English speakers do not have, and the ability to speak more than one language is valued in many arenas. Teachers should be aware that the prior knowledge that such students possess is viewed differently by the mainstream culture.

Another point about background knowledge that teachers should remember is that the background knowledge of each student is unique. Every student has different background knowledge—English speakers, Spanish speakers, and bilingual students. Background knowledge is developed through life experiences, family interactions, the media, play experiences, and so on. Students who are English speaking will not have the same experiences and so will not have the same background knowledge. They may share some common experiences, but each student will have unique views and ideas.

Some teachers intuitively think that all Spanish-speaking students will have the same kinds of background experiences. The Spanish-speaking students in the classroom may have common experiences, just as English-speaking students do, but they also may vary considerably. Just as English-speaking students from different areas of the country have different backgrounds, speakers of Spanish do as well. For example, a student who lives in Minnesota has many experiences different from those of a student who lives in Florida. The student from Minnesota will have had many more experiences with cold and snow, and the student from Florida will have had many more experiences with warm weather and possibly the ocean. The same holds true with Spanish speakers. Students from Bolivia will have experiences very different from those of students from Mexico. Therefore, teachers should remember that all students, whether they speak English, Spanish, or are bilingual, will have unique life experiences that will have an impact on their reading comprehension.

Teachers also come to school with their own background knowledge, and the most common background experience of teachers is being a middle class white woman (National Center for Educational Statistics, 2001). The background of the white middle class, therefore, tends to be the one transmitted in school (Gee, 1996). Teachers need to recognize that their own background knowledge is culturally developed and that they may need to move outside their own comfort levels to provide students with texts that align more closely with their life experiences rather than always asking students to align their thinking with that of the teacher.

In order to help students comprehend text, teachers need to help students access the background knowledge they have, and if the topic of the text is unfamiliar to them, teachers should help students expand their prior knowledge before reading. Taking the time to encourage students to think about a topic before reading can help students comprehend the text they are reading.

Students can develop background knowledge through technology.

Continental Book Company
www.continentalbook.com
A resource center for different types of literature that specializes in Spanish, ESL, French, German, and Italian.

2.1 Teaching Strategy 1

Group Frame

A Group Frame (Brechtel, 1992) is a strategy that provides students with a venue for sharing their ideas about a topic in their dominant language and/or their second language before reading. After students have volunteered their thoughts, the teacher can scaffold the students' knowledge so that it aligns more closely with the text that they will be reading. The teacher's role is to help students access the background knowledge they have about the topic, and then to clarify and expand their initial understandings of concepts before they read the text.

DIRECTIONS AND EXAMPLES

1. Identify a topic that is central to a text that you are reading or that students will be reading. If you are reading a fictional text, identify one or more topics that will help students understand the story. For example, if you are reading *The Three Little Javelinas* in English (Lowell, 1992b) or *Los tres pequeños jabalíes* in Spanish (Lowell, 1992a) to the class you will first want to make sure that all students are familiar with the "Three Little Pigs" tale. Either tell the students the story of the "Three Little Pigs" yourself or have students tell their versions of the story. Once students understand that *The Three Little Javelinas* is an adaptation of the "Three Little Pigs," choose the topic from the book that is most necessary for comprehension—in this case, the desert.

2. Develop a question about the topic. Explain to students that you will be asking them a question that relates to the book that they will be reading. Write the question on the chalkboard. A question about the topic "desert" that applies to *The Three Little Javelinas* follows.

What do you know about the desert?

3. Divide the class into groups of three or four students. If you are teaching the class in English, make sure that a proficient English speaker is in each group. If you are teaching the class in Spanish, make sure that a proficient Spanish speaker is in each group. Tell students to answer the question by discussing anything they know about the desert.

4. After students have discussed the question, ask them to share their ideas with the class. Write the ideas as complete sentences on the board or on an overhead transparency as in the following example.

Dictated Sentences in English	Dictated Sentences in Spanish
The desert is hot.	El desierto es caluroso.
You can see cactus in the desert.	Puedes ver cactus en el desierto.
The desert has lots of sand.	El desierto tiene mucha arena.
There is no water in the desert.	No hay agua en el desierto.

5. Explain to students that their ideas represent what they know about the desert right now and that this knowledge is their background knowledge. Tell students that they have accessed their background knowledge before reading and that by doing so they will understand the story better.

6. Emphasize to students that the knowledge they have about a subject is important and valuable but that sometimes their ideas are a bit different from school knowledge. Explain that the knowledge students learn in school is one kind of learning and that this learning may be different from the kinds of things they learn at home.

7. Explain to students that school learning is important for them to understand because school learning can help them succeed in the mainstream culture. Then tell students that you are going to help them expand their background knowledge by revising the ideas they have about the desert.
8. Use the sentences students dictated to scaffold them about the topic as in the example that follows.

Revised Sentences in English	Revised Sentences in Spanish
The desert is hot during the day in the summer. The nights and winters can be cool.	El desierto es caluroso durante el día en el verano. Las noches y los inviernos pueden ser frescos.
Cacti are one of the "trees" of the desert. There are also other trees that grow in dry climates.	Los cactus son uno de los "árboles" del desierto. También hay otros árboles que crecen en climas secos.
The soil in the desert is sandy.	El suelo del desierto es arenoso.
There is little rainfall in the desert.	Hay poca lluvia en el desierto.

9. Have students read the revised sentences and discuss with students the ways in which you clarified facts about the topic. Tell students that they now know more about the desert and that these new ideas form expanded background knowledge that they can use as they read or hear *The Three Little Javelinas.*
10. Tell students that they should try to access their background knowledge before they read any text.

11. Group Frame reproducibles that you can use with your English or Spanish class follow on pages 20–21.

ASSESSMENT IDEA

As students discuss their ideas during a Group Frame, you can assess their oral language proficiency by listening to them and noting whether or not the students are using words appropriately and whether they are using the grammar of the language of instruction. If you notice any student that exhibits unusual difficulty, make a note of it and develop instruction to provide the student with opportunities to hear and speak the language.

GROUP FRAME

Dictated Sentences in English	Revised Sentences in English

GROUP FRAME

Oraciones dictados en español	Oraciones dictados en español

<table>
<tr><td>

2.1 Teaching Strategy 2

</td><td>

K-W-L

One of the most popular strategies for all students to access and develop their background knowledge of informational text is the K-W-L strategy (Ogle, 1986). The K-W-L strategy represents three processes that students should use as they approach texts: 1) think about what they know, 2) think about what they want to know, and 3) think about what they have learned after they have read the text. The letters K-W-L, therefore, stand for Know, Want to know, and Learned.

</td></tr>
</table>

Teachers can use the K-W-L strategy in a number of ways. Teachers can use a K-W-L as a method for having the entire class discuss a theme or issue that they will be studying; they can use the K-W-L as an organizational tool for individual students; and they can use the K-W-L as a means to have students share common background knowledge. When used in a group, K-W-L is an effective strategy for developing background knowledge. Used in any of these ways, K-W-L is a useful strategy for both speakers of English and speakers of Spanish.

DIRECTIONS AND EXAMPLES

1. Tell students that they will be reading about a subject for which they have some background knowledge. By saying something like the statements that follow, you can remind students that when they read they should access their background knowledge.

   > When you read, you should try to think about what you know about the topic. Today we're going to read a book about dinosaurs. You may think that you know very little about this subject, but you really do have some background knowledge about it. Before you read this topic, you should try to remember whatever you can about dinosaurs.

2. Inform students that there is a reading strategy called K-W-L that can help them organize their thoughts as they access background knowledge. Tell students that K-W-L stands for what they already know, what they want to learn, and what they have learned after reading. Explain to students that they will be working on the K section and the W section before reading and the L section after reading.

3. Show students the book they will be reading for which they will use the K-W-L strategy and distribute the appropriate reproducible on pages 25–26. Use the English version if students will be learning about the subject in English and the Spanish version if students will be learning in Spanish.

4. Ask students what they know about the topic, in this case dinosaurs. Have students discuss dinosaurs in small groups. As you form the groups, make sure that proficient speakers of the language are in each group. Provide directions as in the following statements.

   > Think about what you know about dinosaurs. You may not have read any books about them, but you may know more than you think. You may have heard about dinosaurs from other students; or you may have seen something about dinosaurs on television. Try to remember what you already know about dinosaurs.

5. Tell students that one person in their group should be assigned the task of writing the group's comments on the K-W-L sheet. You might assign that task, or you could have students select one of the group's participants to be the recorder. The recorder should be a proficient writer of the language in which you are teaching.

6. Give students ample time to discuss the topic and record what they already know. When each of the groups has recorded some information, bring the small groups together to engage in whole-class discussion. Have all students share what they already know, not just the students who recorded the ideas. Your goal should be to involve as many students as possible in the discussion so that new ideas become part of those students' background knowledge in the language you're using for discussion. As students talk about dinosaurs in English, for example, they will be more able to read and comprehend the English book *Dinosaurs* (Dorling Kindersley, 1991). If you are teaching in Spanish and students are reading the book *Dinosaurios* (Editorial Sigmar, 1993), you will want them to discuss in Spanish so that they develop their background knowledge and vocabulary about dinosaurs in Spanish.

7. An example of the K section of the K-W-L follows.

What I Know About Dinosaurs

They were big.

They lived a long time ago.

Some dinosaurs are Stegosaurus, Tyrannosaurus Rex, and Brontosaurus.

There are no dinosaurs alive right now.

There are many stories in my culture about big animals that could have been dinosaurs.

Some people think dinosaurs were monsters.

Some dinosaurs ate plants and some ate other animals.

8. Show students pictures or models of dinosaurs or have them page through the book *Dinosaurs* so that they can visualize these large animals. Remember that some students may have heard about dinosaurs but never have seen pictures of them. For other students dinosaurs may be a new topic of learning. Spend ample time helping students develop and access their background knowledge before reading.

9. After class discussion and developing background knowledge by showing pictures or models, have students write what they now know about dinosaurs on their K-W-L sheets. Emphasize to students that they now know more about dinosaurs.

10. Since all students now have some knowledge about dinosaurs, ask them what else they want to learn about the topic. Explain to students that before they read any piece of informational text they should ask themselves what it is that they hope to learn. Model this part of the K-W-L by saying something like the following statements.

I know some things about dinosaurs but there are many other things I really want to know. I want to know what kinds of dinosaurs lived on earth and whether they lived at the same time as people. I also want to know why we don't see dinosaurs anymore. I'm not sure whether this book will answer my questions, and if it doesn't, I can read other books.

11. Ask students to think about what they want to know about dinosaurs. Have students form groups once again to discuss what they want to learn. Have students write their questions on the W section of the appropriate K-W-L reproducible.

12. Discuss the questions that students want to have answered in whole-class discussion. These discussions can also develop the background knowledge of individual students and add to their knowledge base. Develop a class list of questions as in the following example.

What I Want to Learn

What are the types of dinosaurs?

How did dinosaurs live?

What did they look like?

Did they live when people did?

Are any dinosaurs alive today?

13. Have students read the book *Dinosaurs* in English or *Dinosaurios* in Spanish or read the book to students. If students are able to read this book independently or in small groups, give them time to read it once for an overall impression then a second time to answer the questions on the K-W-L chart.

14. After the book has been read, ask students what they have learned. Have them work in groups once again to record their ideas on the L portion of the K-W-L chart.

15. Share what students have learned by discussing their learning in a whole-group discussion. Record what students say on the L portion of the chart as in the following example.

What I Learned

Tyrannosaurs Rex ate small animals.

The Triceratops had horns and armor.

They hatched from eggs.

16. Discuss with students whether what they learned from this book answered their questions. If their questions were not answered, encourage students to learn more about the topic.

17. Remind students to always access their background knowledge before they read.

NAME _____ DATE _____

K-W-L STRATEGY

Topic _____

What I Already Know About the Topic

_____
_____
_____
_____
_____
_____

What I Want to Know About the Topic

_____
_____
_____
_____
_____
_____

What I Have Learned About the Topic after Reading

_____
_____
_____
_____
_____
_____

NOMBRE _____ FECHA _____

K-W-L STRATEGY

Tema _____

Lo Que Ya Sé Acerca del Tema

_____

_____

_____

_____

_____

_____

Lo Que Quiero Saber Acerca del Tema

_____

_____

_____

_____

_____

_____

Lo Que He Aprendido Acerca del Tema Después de Leer

_____

_____

_____

_____

_____

_____

2.1 **Teaching Strategy 3**

Anticipation Guide

Students can access background knowledge before reading in a number of ways. They can remember factual information, and they can also think about memories, opinions, and anecdotes. One strategy that encourages students to think about ideas and concepts, rather than facts, is the Anticipation Guide (Herber, 1978). An Anticipation Guide is a set of prereading questions that have students form opinions about the themes of the story they will be reading. An Anticipation Guide is especially valuable for students who are learning a new language. Students can access ideas and memories in either their first or second language or can discuss them before reading. During discussions, though, students should remain in the language of instruction.

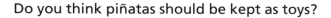

DIRECTIONS AND EXAMPLE

1. Select a story that you will read to the class or that students will read independently.
2. Identify one or more themes from that selection. Pose the theme in a question that can be answered with a "yes" or a "no" and write it on the chalkboard. An example from the bilingual book *The Perfect Piñata: La piñata perfecta* (Dominguez, 2002) follows.

Do you think piñatas should be kept as toys?

3. Divide the class into small groups and ask students to discuss the question. Make sure that each group has at least one student who is proficient in the language of instruction. Tell students to answer the question with a "yes" or a "no" and give reasons for their answers. Encourage students to converse with each other and to tell each other stories they know about piñatas.
4. After students have discussed the question, have them share their opinions with the entire class. Remind students that there is not one right answer but that each person's opinion is valuable. A sample classroom discussion follows.

TEACHER:	Who answered this question with a "no"? Carlos, what did you think?
CARLOS:	I think that piñatas are made so that you can get the candy inside.
TEACHER:	Then you disagree that piñatas should be kept as toys.
CARLOS:	Right. I don't think piñatas should be kept as toys. My cousin wanted to keep her piñata when we had her birthday, but none of the rest of us did. We wanted the candy.
TEACHER:	Who else answered the question with a "no"?
EMILY:	I agree with Carlos. I think the reason piñatas are made is so that you can open them up. I've never heard of anyone wanting to keep a piñata to play with.
TEACHER:	Great. Now who has a different opinion? Who thinks that piñatas could be kept as toys?

SOFIA:	I do. My grandma has a piñata from when she was a girl that she keeps in her bedroom. It's a very beautiful donkey piñata from Mexico. She said that it reminds her of her village and she won't let anyone open it. It's not a toy, but she keeps it like it's a precious doll.
TEACHER:	That's a good example, Sofia. Who else has a story to tell about piñatas?

5. After discussing the question with students, tell them that they will be reading a story about the topic of the Anticipation Guide question. Remind students that they accessed their background knowledge before reading by their discussion. Tell students that each time they read they should read the title of the story and try to remember their experiences that relate to the story's ideas. Explain to students that they can access their background knowledge continually as they read.

6. Reproducible Anticipation Guides in English and Spanish follow on pages 29–30.

VARIATION

Anticipation Guides can also be used to help students access factual background knowledge. If you are teaching a unit on space, for example, you could develop a list of statements to which students could answer "yes" or "no," such as "There are nine planets." When students discuss these factual statements, they also are accessing their background knowledge and remembering what they know. It's important, however, for students to have the opportunity to discuss their ideas in groups before reading. When students discuss with other students, they are able to remember more things than if working alone. Conversations are especially important when students are learning a new language.

NAME _____ DATE _____

ANTICIPATION GUIDE

Title of Story _____

Author _____

Yes   No   1. _____

_____

Yes   No   2. _____

_____

Yes   No   3. _____

_____

Yes   No   4. _____

_____

Yes   No   5. _____

_____

Yes   No   6. _____

_____

NOMBRE _____ FECHA _____

ANTICIPATION GUIDE

Título de la Historia _____

Autor _____

Sí   No   1. _____

_____

Sí   No   2. _____

_____

Sí   No   3. _____

_____

Sí   No   4. _____

_____

Sí   No   5. _____

_____

Sí   No   6. _____

_____

SECTION 2.2 Developing Vocabulary

> *Instructional Goal:* **To help students become familiar with word meanings before reading so they can comprehend texts**

BACKGROUND

Words are the foundation pieces of language, so the knowledge of words and word meanings is essential for successful communication in both English and Spanish. Students for whom English or Spanish is their first language acquire thousands of words by listening to their caretakers talk and discuss household events. Actually, this is true of native speakers of any language. Think of all of the talk that occurs during a typical evening in an English-speaking or Spanish-speaking household. Those conversations—the words themselves and the grammar that is used—become ingrained in the minds of the children. These children, then, have hours and hours of experiences listening to their first language outside of school.

Think about what it means to learn a second language. For students who depend on the school to acquire their second language, the input they receive at school may be the only input they receive at all. In addition to this, students may have entirely different outside experiences, which will have a definite impact on their knowledge of the words they are trying to learn as their second language. Students who hear Spanish at home are learning the foundations of Spanish and are developing their vocabularies in Spanish, the same way English-speaking students are learning vocabularies in English. Regardless of the language being learned/acquired (i.e., English or Spanish), students need to know function words, or words that cannot be defined, such as the linking verb "to be." These words are best learned as sight words. Words that are not abstract and that have definitions, however, should be taught as vocabulary words.

For comprehension of texts, students do not need to be able to define all of the words that they encounter; they need to be able to discern the word's meaning in the context. Baumann, Kame'enui, and Ash (2003) divide vocabulary into two types of language learning: expressive (speaking or writing) and receptive (reading and listening). When students read, they need to have developed some concept of the word, but to use the word in speaking or writing, they need to remember and retrieve the word, a skill that is much more sophisticated.

The difficulty with teaching students new vocabulary in any given language—even within the same language—is that most children have different background knowledge about words and concepts. For example, a third-grade student who has recently immigrated from a small village in Mexico might have no experience with zoos. A story or unit on zoos might be difficult, even if the word "zoo" has been defined for the student. Since vocabulary is learned through applying background knowledge to learn word meanings and concepts, Spanish-speaking students may need to increase their background knowledge about a topic as they are learning new words. Another example may relate to speakers of the same language who have mastered a different dialect of that

How can Manuel develop his English vocabulary?

language. In some cases, a given word may have a totally different denotation. For example, native speakers of Chilean Spanish use the word "guagua" to refer to a "baby" while native speakers of Puerto Rican Spanish use "guagua" to refer to a "bus" or "truck." In this case, the same word denotes different images in the readers' minds. The same is true among native speakers of English due to dialectological differences. Additionally, some speakers may totally lack background knowledge due to limited real world experiences or different experiences. Thus, some vocabulary words will be entirely new to both your English-speaking and Spanish-speaking students. When this is the case, you'll need to help all students develop background knowledge about the topic.

For students to be successful learning new words, they need to learn in meaningful contexts (Jiménez, 2001). When students understand why they need to learn word meanings and they can apply their knowledge to situations of importance, they develop their vocabularies more rapidly.

The instructional strategies in this section are designed to be used by teachers before students read a selection of text so that students learn word definitions, develop a conceptual understanding of words, rate their knowledge of word meanings, and predict how words will be used in a piece of reading. All of these cognitive strategies will help students as they develop their vocabularies and become proficient enough in their new language to comprehend texts.

Literacy Connection Resources
www.literacyconnections.com/secondlanguage.html
Bilingual, Spanish, and ESL literacy resources. Includes Spanish resources, music, and games to teach English as a second language.

2.2 Teaching Strategy 4

Vocabulary Four Square

Vocabulary Four Square has been described as both a prereading and an after reading vocabulary activity for English-speaking students of all ages (e.g., Lenski, Wham, & Johns, 2003). Vocabulary Four Square is also an ideal strategy for Spanish-speaking students, or students who are learning any language, so this strategy can be used in bilingual classrooms as well as monolingual classrooms. When students learn the meanings of vocabulary words with Vocabulary Four Square, they not only learn the definitions of words, but they also develop conceptual knowledge about the words through connecting word meanings to familiar words and background experiences. This strategy is especially useful for students who are new to the culture represented by their school.

DIRECTIONS AND EXAMPLE

1. Identify several vocabulary words that you want students to learn. Choose words for this strategy that are not function words (i.e., high-frequency

words that are abstract such as "the") but have definitions that students can understand.

2. Tell students that they will be learning the meanings of some new words. Write the new words on the board and pronounce them for students. For example, if you were reading the bilingual book *Uncle Nacho's Hat: El sombrero del tío Nacho* (Rohmer, 1989), a book printed in both Spanish and English, you might choose the following vocabulary words to teach.

English	Spanish
Visit	Visita
Trunk	Baúl
Trash	Basura
Market	Mercado
Thief	Ladrón
Full of holes	Todo agujereado

3. Use either the English example or the Spanish example that follows to model the strategy. Read the labels in each of the four quadrants. You might need to define the words the first few times you use the strategy. Explain to students that you will be demonstrating how they will use the Vocabulary Four Square strategy but that they will need to learn how to use it independently in time.

VOCABULARY FOUR SQUARE

Vocabulary Word	What It's Like
Trunk	*Suitcase* *Luggage*
What It Means	**Personal Connections**
Large container used to store things	*Place to store mementos* *Large black box in basement*

VOCABULARY FOUR SQUARE

Palabra	Se Parece a
Baúl	*Maleta* *Equipaje*
Lo Que Significa	**En lo Personal, me Recuerda**
Contenedor para guardar cosas	*Lugar para guardar recuerdos* *Caja grande y negra en el sótano*

4. Write one of the new vocabulary words in the upper left-hand quadrant under the label *Vocabulary Word* or *Palabra.* Read the word with students and have them read it aloud with you several times. Instruct students to write the word in the square.

5. Divide the class into groups of three or four students. Regardless of the language in which you are teaching, ensure that there is/are always one or two students in each group whose proficiency is higher than their peer's. Students who have advanced proficiency in any language can model the strategy to those less proficient in that same language. Then ask students to tell their classmates what they know about the meanings of the words. Reassure students by telling them that they might know a partial definition and that they should discuss what they know.

6. Ask students to volunteer their knowledge of the meanings of the words. If students give a meaning that fits the context of the story, write it in the blank *What It Means* or *Lo Que Significa.* If students are unable to define the word, provide a definition yourself.

7. In the upper right-hand quadrant, have students write words and phrases that expand their definition. Tell students to notice the label *What It's Like* or *Se Parece a.* Explain to students that they should think of other ways to describe the vocabulary word. For example, if you were teaching the word "trunk," you might write the words "suitcase," "baggage," and "luggage." These new words have slightly different connotations, but their meanings are similar to the word "trunk." If you are teaching this lesson in English, Spanish-speaking students might want to include some Spanish words in this section. Determine how many Spanish words students can use based on your instructional goals.

8. In the lower right-hand quadrant, have students write personal connections or associations to the word under the label *Personal Connections* or *En lo Personal, me Recuerda.* Remind students that they will remember new vocabulary words more rapidly if they connect them to their personal background knowledge. Then, have students think about any connections they can make to the new word. In order to make your example comprehensible to your language learners, be sure to display your example on an overhead transparency or by means of any other visual display.

9. Demonstrate how to make connections by using your own experience or by making the following statements.

> The word "trunk" means a large container or suitcase that can be used to store items. We have a black trunk in our basement that my grandparents used to store mementos from their home. When I think about the word "trunk," I picture the dusty, black trunk. In this box, I'll write "place to store mementos" and "large black box."

10. Duplicate and distribute one of the Vocabulary Four Square reproducibles on pages 36–37. Use either the English example or the Spanish example.

11. Model Vocabulary Four Square several times with the class until they feel comfortable using the strategy independently or in small groups. When students are confident that they can work alone, give them a copy of the reproducible to complete for each new word. Be especially aware of the

progress of language learners who are new to the country. Provide all students assistance until they are successful learning new words with this strategy.

12. Have students use completed Vocabulary Four Square sheets to review the words they have learned. Remind students that they may need to practice a word as many as 30 times before they know it well enough to use in speaking or writing.

13. As often as possible, encourage students to use all new words they have learned in their speaking. Explain to students that they will learn their second language (i.e., English or Spanish) more rapidly if they practice the new words frequently.

VARIATION

You can change the labels on the four quadrants based on the age of your students and their language proficiency. Students just learning a second language are often helped if you include an illustration. The illustration can be presented next to the word. The illustration often helps students cement their knowledge of the word's meaning. To meet the needs of learners who are more advanced in their language development/acquisition process, you may consider it more challenging to provide an antonym for the given term in the box for *Personal Connections*. For instance, for students who are gaining proficiency in English or students who are native English speakers, you should consider changing the label *Personal Connections* to *Opposites*. In this quadrant students should write examples of words or phrases that are different from the vocabulary word. When students think of ideas that are opposite to the word they are learning, they enlarge their conceptual understanding of that word.

ASSESSMENT IDEA

The Vocabulary Four Square can also be used as an assessment tool. When students are familiar with a word's meaning, you can give them the Vocabulary Four Square reproducible to assess their conceptual knowledge of the word. This type of assessment is much more comprehensive than merely asking students to give a definition for a word.

NAME _____ DATE _____

VOCABULARY FOUR SQUARE

Vocabulary Word	What It's Like
What It Means	**Personal Connections**

Vocabulary Word	What It's Like
What It Means	**Personal Connections**

NOMBRE _____ FECHA _____

VOCABULARY FOUR SQUARE

Palabra	Se Parece a
Lo Que Significa	**En lo Personal, me Recuerda**

Palabra	Se Parece a
Lo Que Significa	**En lo Personal, me Recuerda**

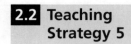

Knowledge Rating Scale

The Knowledge Rating Scale (Blachowicz, 1986) is a strategy that helps students apply their background knowledge to vocabulary words to determine whether the words are in their receptive lexicons, expressive lexicons, or in neither. As students discuss their knowledge of words in small groups, they add to their conceptual understanding of words so that they have a richer knowledge of all words simply by participating in the strategy. Students who are English speakers should complete the strategy in English as it was developed. Spanish speakers should complete the strategy in Spanish. The Knowledge Rating Scale is appropriate for use before students hear or read a piece of literature, before a unit of study, and as a prereading activity for other texts.

DIRECTIONS

1. Identify a book that contains words that are unfamiliar to most of the students. Choose six to eight words from the book for the strategy. Some of the words should be unfamiliar to most students, but two or three words should be somewhat familiar to all students.
2. The examples that follow are based on *Momma, Do You Love Me?* (Joose, 1991a) and *Me quieres, mamá* (Joose, 1991b). Duplicate the English version or the Spanish version of the Knowledge Rating Scale on pages 40–41 and distribute it to students.
3. Point out the words in the left column of the table. Tell students that these words will be important for them to know as they listen to the story so that they can understand what's happening. Explain to students that they will be discussing how well they know the words before hearing the story.
4. Divide the class into groups of three or four students. If all students are participating in the English version, select mixed-language groups.

MAMMA, DO YOU LOVE ME?			
	Know it	*Seen or heard it*	*No clue!*
Salmon			
Mukluks			
Moon			
Polar bear			
Teeth			
Puffin			

¿ME QUIERES, MAMÁ?			
	Lo sé	Lo he visto o escuchado	¡No tengo idea!
Salmón			
Botas de piel de foca			
Luna			
Oso polar			
Dientes			
Frailecillo			

5. Ask students to discuss their knowledge of the words and check the portion of the Knowledge Rating Scale that represents their knowledge. For example, if they really know what the word means, can use the word in a sentence, and give a definition, they know it well. If students do not know the word but have seen it or heard it, have them mark the *Seen or Heard It* column. If the word is entirely unfamiliar, they should mark *No Clue!*

6. After students have rated their knowledge of the words, either read the story or tell them what the unfamiliar words mean. Show pictures where appropriate. For example, the meaning of "mukluks" can be much better understood if you show students the picture. Use the Knowledge Rating Scale reproducibles on pages 40–41 to develop additional lessons. Use the English version or the Spanish version where appropriate.

VARIATION

If you are working in a dual language environment (either one- or two-way) have Spanish-speaking students notice the similarities between the English word "salmon" and the Spanish word "salmón." Have students come up with similar examples. Remind students that many words contain the same word chunks in English and in Spanish. Point out other similar words in the story such as "parka" and "lemmings." Tell students that not all words that seem similar have the same meaning but many of them do. Remind students that words spelled the same in both languages often have different pronunciations.

On the other hand, some words that originated in English may have a translation into Spanish that could be confusing if students try to translate the word back into Spanish. For example, the Spanish word for "puffin," a black and white seabird that is found in the Northern Hemisphere, is "frailecillo," which means "little priest" in Spanish. Remind students that when they learn vocabulary words in English their Spanish translations can be unusual and sometimes humorous.

NAME _____ DATE _____

KNOWLEDGE RATING SCALE

	Know it	Seen or heard it	No clue!

From Blachowicz, C. L. Z. (1986). Making connections: Alternative to the vocabulary notebook. *Journal of Reading, 29*, 643–649.

NOMBRE _____ FECHA _____

KNOWLEDGE RATING SCALE

	Lo sé	Lo he visto o escuchado	¡No tengo idea!

Based on Blachowicz, C. L. Z. (1986). Making connections: Alternative to the vocabulary notebook. *Journal of Reading*, *29*, 643–649.

From Susan Davis Lenski and Fabiola Ehlers-Zavala, *Reading Strategies for Spanish Speakers*. Copyright © 2004 by Kendall/Hunt Publishing Company (1-800-247-3458). May be reproduced for noncommercial educational purposes.

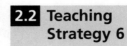

2.2 Teaching Strategy 6

Possible Sentences

As students prepare to read, they should think about the text and make predictions about the content. Possible Sentences (Moore & Moore, 1992) is a strategy that has students talk about new words, predict a sentence that they think could occur in the text that includes two or more key words, and read to confirm their predictions. Possible Sentences should be used for words that are in students' receptive vocabulary so that they can make predictions about the words' meanings.

Possible Sentences is a fun activity for students and a valuable one. When students compose sentences that contain new words, they expand the boundaries of their knowledge about the words and about the text's topic. When this happens, students are given the opportunity to use new words in discussion with their peers, they learn the vocabulary terms, and they reinforce their sentence structure skills. Further, Possible Sentences, along with many prediction strategies, often arouses students' curiosity about the words, the texts, and the topic.

DIRECTIONS AND EXAMPLES

1. Identify words or phrases that may be in students' receptive vocabulary that you want to reinforce. These are words that students may have heard before and have an idea about their definitions. Choose 7 to 10 words.

2. List the words on a board or on an overhead transparency. If you were having students read *The Giver* by Lois Lowry (1993b), for example, you might choose the following words for students to learn.

> Cargo plane
>
> Rasping
>
> Nurturer
>
> Learning community
>
> Guilt
>
> Apprehensive
>
> Patriotic hymn

3. If students are reading the book in Spanish, *El dador* (Lowry, 1993a), you should list the words in Spanish.

> Aviones de carga
>
> Rasposa
>
> Criador
>
> Comunidad escolar
>
> Culpa
>
> Intranquilo
>
> Canto patriótico

4. Tell students the title of the text they will be reading and a bit about the text. In the example of *The Giver*, you would present something like the following introduction.

> **You are going to start a new book today, a novel titled *The Giver*. In this story, you'll meet Jonas who lives in a world where everything is under control and the people are given no choices. The first chapter of the book describes the first time in Jonas's life that he was frightened.**

5. Duplicate and distribute one of the reproducibles on pages 44–45. Choose the English or the Spanish reproducible depending on the language that the students are using to read the text.
6. Tell students that they will encounter the words listed on the board in their reading of the first chapter of *The Giver*. Divide the class into groups of three or four students and have them share their understandings of the words listed.

7. Then ask students to compose four sentences that could possibly be written in the text, each that uses two or more of the listed words. Have students write these sentences on the bottom portion of the reproducible. Explain to students that they should think of sentences that could actually have been written by Lois Lowry. Students can compose these sentences in groups or independently. Demonstrate an example sentence such as the one that follows.

> **Jonas was <u>distracted</u> by the <u>cargo plane</u> that made a <u>rasping</u> sound overhead.**

8. After students have written their sentences, have them share some of the sentences with the class. Write two or three sample sentences on the board.
9. Instruct students to read the selection, in this case chapter 1 of *The Giver*. Tell them that as they read they should determine whether the sentences they have written are similar to any sentences or thoughts in the actual book. Score the sentences by grading them with a "T" for "True," "F" for "False," and "DK" for "Don't Know."
10. Correct inaccurate sentences so that they conform to the text.

VARIATION

Possible Sentences is a strategy that works extremely well for content area texts, such as science and social studies. Often these textbooks have vocabulary words listed in front of a chapter. Encourage students to predict what the listed words mean and how they are used.

NAME _____ DATE _____

POSSIBLE SENTENCES

_____

Title of Text

Below are some words that you will find in your reading.

_____   _____

_____   _____

_____   _____

_____   _____

_____   _____

Write one or more sentences using at least two of the above words in each sentence. Underline the words you use from the list above. After reading, rate the sentences by using the following key.

T = True   **F = False**   **DK = Don't Know**

_____ 1. _____

_____

_____ 2. _____

_____

_____ 3. _____

_____

_____ 4. _____

_____

NOMBRE _____ FECHA _____

POSSIBLE SENTENCES

Título

Abajo hay algunas palabras que aparecerán en tu lectura.

_____   _____
_____   _____
_____   _____
_____   _____
_____   _____

Escribe una o más oraciones usando por lo menos dos de las palabras que aparecen arriba en cada oración. Subraya las palabras que has utilizado de la lista. Luego de leer, decide si cada oración es verdadera (V), falsa (F), or si no lo sabes (NS). Utiliza la siguiente pauta.

V = Verdadera   **F = Falsa**   **NS = No sé**

_____ 1. _____

_____

_____ 2. _____

_____

_____ 3. _____

_____

_____ 4. _____

_____

45

SECTION 2.3   # Identifying Text Structure

Instructional Goal: **To teach students how to use text structure to increase comprehension**

BACKGROUND

All texts are organized in culturally accepted ways. In English-speaking North America, texts tend to be divided into two categories: fictional and informational texts. Fictional texts are stories with a plot that directs the narrative toward a goal. Informational texts can be divided in a number of ways but often have attributive or enumerative patterns, which state a main idea that lists supporting details. These text structures are the most predominant in the United States and Canada, and because they are so common, students who are knowledgeable about these text structures tend to have better comprehension when reading English texts.

Students who have been raised in mainstream English-speaking families and have heard stories told to them or read to them will have a good understanding of fictional text structure. Stein and Glenn (1979) found that young children could identify the plot, setting, and characters of stories even when they had not had instruction on these story elements. As these students read fictional texts, then, they can use their knowledge about the story structure to store, retrieve, and summarize information (Meyer, Brandt, & Bluth, 1980). These abilities with the structure of a language, along with understanding the setting, role of participants, and register, are among the skills necessary to be competent in a language (Hadaway, Vardell, & Young, 2002).

When students have not been exposed to the text structures common in the United States and Canada, they may have a difficult time following the story line.

Ramón is helping Juan understand how this story is organized.

Furthermore, many Spanish books have been originally published in English and then translated into Spanish. These books, for the most part, will still contain a story line that is more typical of English texts than Spanish texts. Conversely, students who are in dual language programs, are native English speakers, and are learning Spanish may have difficulty reading texts that originated in the Spanish language. Many Spanish stories follow a more circular route than do English stories; and Spanish informational texts tend to follow nonlinear reasoning rather than being direct. For these reasons, both English and Spanish language learners may need instruction about text structure (Peregoy & Boyle, 2001). The strategies that follow in this section were developed so that students who are learning English can follow the structures of English texts.

The Literacy Center
www.literacycenter.net
Gives lessons in different languages including English, Spanish, German, and French.

Pacific Learning
www.pacificlearning.com
Gives names of books for early readers and fluent readers in English and Spanish.

2.3 **Teaching Strategy 7**

Previewing Texts

Before they begin to read, students need to look at texts to determine whether these texts are narrative or informational. They can do this by previewing the texts and locating the textual cues that signal text structure. If students preview texts, think about the text structure before they read, and recall their prior knowledge about text structure, they will be able to make more sense of their reading.

DIRECTIONS AND EXAMPLES

1. Tell students that you are going to give them ideas about what to think about before they begin to read. Explain that different groups of people tell stories differently. You might say something like the following example.

   > Books by English authors typically have a certain pattern. This pattern may not be the same as the pattern your grandfather uses when he tells you a story or the pattern of television programs you watch in Spanish. But you'll notice that television programs, books, and stories in English all follow the same pattern. They begin with an introduction to the characters, and then a problem is introduced and is solved.

2. Give an example of a different pattern of a story that is typical of your region or the culture of the people who live in your area.
3. Explain the story structure of informational texts that are written in English. Explain to students that informational texts usually are very straightforward, giving main ideas first and then supporting details. Give an example of a passage of informational text that uses this pattern as in the following example.

   > Tropical rain forests are areas of land that are warm, with a high amount of rainfall. In tropical rain forests, the ferns and trees grow abundantly, so close together that they form a canopy overhead. The canopy is closed, meaning that the trees obscure the sky, making it dark and gloomy. The air is steamy and moist. Rain forests are noisy with a cacophony of sounds: birds screeching, monkeys chattering, insects buzzing, and frogs croaking. Trails become overgrown in a matter of days because of the warm weather and daily rain.

4. Tell students that this pattern may be different from the kinds of informational texts they read in Spanish. If your students are proficient Spanish speakers and have had previous experiences with texts that originated in Spanish, show them an example of a Spanish text that is not as linear and direct as the English text. Explain to students that Spanish writing uses a different pattern for informational texts. Emphasize to students that it's important to learn the textual patterns of both cultures to be proficient in both English and Spanish.

5. Select an informational book and a piece of fiction. For this activity, select books that are in English or Spanish depending on the language of instruction. If you are teaching in Spanish, select books for this activity that have been written in English and then translated into Spanish. Books that originated in Spanish may have a different story structure and should be addressed separately.

6. For the narrative text, conduct a "page walk" through the book. Do this by showing the front cover and each of the pages if the book is short. If you are using a chapter book, show students the front cover and the beginning pages of each chapter. An example from the book *The Kissing Hand* (Penn, 1993a) in English and translated into Spanish as *Un beso en mi mano* (Penn, 1993b) follows.

TEACHER: Let's look at the front cover and think about the title. What do you see on the cover?

STUDENTS: We see a small raccoon and a bigger raccoon.

TEACHER: What is the bigger raccoon doing?

STUDENTS: It's kissing the baby raccoon's hand.

TEACHER: Good, now let's look through the book. What do you see in the first few pictures?

STUDENTS: The baby raccoon seems to be crying and looking sad. It's talking with other animals.

TEACHER: Right. You see a small raccoon that is showing emotion. Do you think the book is fictional or informational?

STUDENTS: The book must be fiction.

7. Discuss with students how they knew that the book was fiction and how they predict the story will progress. Remind students that by previewing texts they can know something about the story before they read.

VARIATION

You can use this strategy with informational books as well. Select an informational book, such as a science book, a social studies book, or a trade book. Duplicate and distribute one of the Previewing Guide reproducibles that follow. Use the English version if the book is written in English and the Spanish version if the book is written in Spanish. Have students answer the questions on the Previewing Guide before reading. Emphasize to students that they need to know about the pattern of the text before reading.

NAME _____ DATE _____

PREVIEWING GUIDE

1. List the title of the book and the name of the author.

   _____

   _____

2. Does the book look like a work of fiction or nonfiction? Why do you think so?

   _____

   _____

   _____

3. Page through the book. What do you notice about the book's pictures, headings, subheading, and graphics?

   _____

   _____

   _____

   _____

   _____

4. What do you predict the book or passage will be about?

   _____

   _____

   _____

   _____

   _____

   _____

NOMBRE _____ FECHA _____

PREVIEWING GUIDE

1. Escribe el título del libro y el nombre del autor.

   _____

   _____

2. ¿Parece el libro de ficción o de la vida real? ¿Por qué piensas eso?

   _____

   _____

   _____

3. Ojea el libro. ¿Qué notas en las fotografías, títulos, subtítulos, y gráficos del libro?

   _____

   _____

   _____

   _____

   _____

4. ¿De qué crees que se tratará el libro o el pasaje de lectura?

   _____

   _____

   _____

   _____

   _____

Predict-O-Gram

A Predict-O-Gram (Blachowicz, 1986) is a prereading strategy that has students predict the ways words and phrases are used in a story. This predicting activity has students decide whether the terms could be used in the elements of the story, or as Ada (2003) calls it "looking within the book." A Predict-O-Gram is a valuable activity for English- or Spanish-language learners for two reasons. First, students discuss new terms in small groups and predict their use in the story. Discussion and prediction about new terms help students expand their definitions of words. Second, students predict in their discussions how terms are used as story elements. The use of the discussion of story grammar can clarify and solidify the meanings of the elements of fiction. This activity is useful for students who are familiar with the story elements common in the English language, and they are especially valuable for students for whom these elements are unfamiliar. When students use Predict-O-Grams, therefore, they learn about the text structure of fictional texts while making predictions about the story.

DIRECTIONS AND EXAMPLES

1. Discuss the story elements that are used in English texts by telling a story that has a typical story structure. Write the story on the chalkboard or tell it orally. You might use the story that follows based on the English or Spanish version of *Stellaluna* (Cannon, 1993a; Cannon 1993b).

   > There once was a bat named Stellaluna who lived in a forest. When he was very small, his mother would carry him as she searched for food. One day an owl attacked his mother and she dropped him. Stellaluna fell through the air and landed in a bird's nest. The mother bird fed Stellaluna with her babies, Pip, Flitter, and Flap. Stellaluna had to eat bugs with the birds and learned how to sit on a branch rather than hang by his legs. He became good friends with the baby birds.
   >
   > When the birds were old enough to fly, Stellaluna took off and soared through the air finding some other bats. These bats laughed at him because he didn't behave like a bat. As Stellaluna was remembering bat behavior, his mother recognized him. Stellaluna was happy about his reunion with his mother and with other bats. He introduced his bird friends to the bats and they all lived together happily.

2. Discuss the main characters of the story, the setting, and the plot with students. An example of a classroom discussion follows.

   TEACHER: The main character of a story is whom the story is about. Who is the main character in this story?

   STUDENT: Stellaluna.

   TEACHER: Yes, Stellaluna is the main character. There are others in the story. Who are they?

   STUDENT: The mother, Pip, Flitter, and Flap.

TEACHER:	Correct. Now where did the story take place? That's called the setting.
STUDENT:	In a forest.
TEACHER:	Yes, now what happened in the plot? The plot is the series of events that take place.
STUDENT:	Stellaluna fell into a nest. The birds raised him. He found his mother and other bats at the end of the story.

3. Tell students to notice the words that signal fictional stories, such as "once upon a time," "There once was . . .," and "happily every after." Tell students that not all fictional stories use these words but that some do.

4. Duplicate and distribute one of the Predict-O-Gram reproducibles that follow. Use the reproducible on page 54 if you are teaching in English and the one on page 55 if you are teaching in Spanish. Tell students that you will be describing a fun strategy for them that will help them learn story structure.

5. Identify words in a story that represent each of the elements of fiction such as the ones listed from the story *Stellaluna*. Write the words on the board for the Predict-O-Gram. Tell students that these words are found in the story *Stellaluna*.

English	**Spanish**
Fruit bat	Murciélago de fruta
Food	Comida
Wings	Alas
Daybreak	Amanecer
Forest	Bosque
Hanging	Colgando
Hungry	Hambriento
Birds	Pájaros
Find mother	Encontrar a mamá
Nest	Nido
Upside down	Al revés
Fly	Volar
Branch	Rama
Baby	Bebé

6. Divide the class into groups of three or four students. Ask students to think about which element of the story the words would fit. Have them write the words in the boxes of the Predict-O-Gram. Examples in both English and Spanish follow.

Setting	**Characters**	**Goal or Problem**
Forest	*Fruit bat*	*Fly*
Daybreak	*Birds*	
	Baby	
Events in the Story	**Solution of the Problem**	**Other Things**
Food	*Find mother*	*Branch*
Hungry		
Upside down		

Ambiente	Personajes	Meta o Problema
Bosque Amanecer	Murciélago de fruta Pájaros Bebé	Volar
Sucesos en la Historia	**Solución del Problema**	**Otras Cosas**
Comida Hambriento Al revés	Encontrar a mamá	Rama

7. Tell students that they can make predictions about a story based on its story structure. Remind students that they should use the structure of a story to help them comprehend as they read.

ASSESSMENT IDEA

You can determine whether students understand story organization by assessing the Predict-O-Grams. Have students explain why they placed each word in a particular category. If students have adequate rationales for their placement of terms, they understand how stories are organized. If students do not have good reasons for the way they placed the words, ask students to think about their choices and try again. If students have difficulty a second time, they need more instruction on the elements of story grammar.

NAME _____ DATE _____

PREDICT-O-GRAM

_____
Title

Directions: Read the words on the lines below and think how they could be used in the story. Write them in the square of the Predict-O-Gram where you think they fit best. You can use more than one word in each square.

_____   _____   _____

_____   _____   _____

_____   _____   _____

_____   _____   _____

Setting	Characters	Goal or Problem
Events in the Story	**Solution of the Problem**	**Other Things**

Based on Blachowicz, C. L. Z. (1986). Making connections: Alternative to the vocabulary notebook. *Journal of Reading*, *29*, 643–649.

From Susan Davis Lenski and Fabiola Ehlers-Zavala, *Reading Strategies for Spanish Speakers*. Copyright © 2004 by Kendall/Hunt Publishing Company (1-800-247-3458). May be reproduced for noncommercial educational purposes.

PREDICT-O-GRAM

_____

Título

Direcciones: Lee las palabras en las siguientes líneas y piensa en como podrían ser usadas en la historia. Escríbelas en el cuadro del Predict-o-Gram donde piensas que encajan mejor. Puedes usar más de una palabra en cada cuadro.

_____   _____   _____
_____   _____   _____
_____   _____   _____
_____   _____   _____

Ambiente	Personajes	Meta o Problema
Sucesos en la Historia	Solución del Problema	Otras Cosas

2.3 **Teaching Strategy 9**

Word Sorts

Similar to a Predict-O-Gram (Blachowicz, 1986) for fictional texts, Word Sorts (Gillet & Kita, 1979) can be used as a prereading strategy to help students think about the text structure for informational texts. The strategy Word Sorts requires students to categorize words, either before or after reading. When used before reading, this activity helps students get a sense of the structure of the text that they will read. This activity is excellent for all students, native speakers of English and students who are learning English. It also is excellent for students who are learning the structures of the Spanish language, whether they are native speakers of Spanish or are learning Spanish as a second language. No matter what language students have as their first language, they will not be familiar with the textual patterns of informational writing. Most students have few experiences with informational text, so they find the patterns common to nonfiction unfamiliar (Yopp & Yopp, 2000).

DIRECTIONS AND EXAMPLES

1. Remind students that informational text in English is typically written with a main idea first, the details next, then the closing statement. Emphasize to students that informational text valued in many Spanish-speaking countries does not use this structure. Explain this concept by saying something like that which follows.

   > When we read informational books in English, they tend to follow a certain pattern. Many times a big idea starts the paragraph or passage, which is called a main idea. After the main idea you will usually find details about the main idea. Then you often find a sentence or a paragraph at the end of the section that restates the main idea.
   >
   > When you read informational books in Spanish, you might find that they follow this same pattern. Some Spanish books we have in school are translated from English and retain the English patterns. Other books we have originated in Spanish. These books probably do not have such a linear way of presenting material. Instead, the information is approached in a nonlinear pattern.
   >
   > There is not a "best" way to write informational text. The United States and Canada use one way. Much of Latin America uses another way. You need to remember which language system to use in each writing situation.

2. Tell students that you will be teaching them a strategy called Word Sorts to help them understand the main idea-detail type of writing. You can use the strategy in English or in Spanish, depending on your language of instruction. If you are using Spanish, however, make sure the texts you are using are written in the English way.

3. Identify a list of words in your text that represent the main idea and details. Write the words on the board. The sample paragraph that was used in Teaching Strategy 7 and a list of words and phrases follow.

Sample Paragraph

Tropical rain forests are areas of land that are warm, with a high amount of rainfall. In tropical rain forests, the ferns and trees grow abundantly, so close together that they form a canopy overhead. The canopy is closed, meaning that the trees obscure the sky, making it dark and gloomy. The air is steamy and moist. Rain forests are noisy with a cacophony of sounds: birds screeching, monkeys chattering, insects buzzing, and frogs croaking. Trails become overgrown in a matter of days because of the warm weather and daily rain.

Word/Phrases List

Rain forest	Canopy	Birds
Areas of land	Dark	Overgrown
High rainfall	Moist	Gloomy
Ferns and trees	Noisy	Insects

4. Have students write each of the words or phrases on the Word Sort Cards on page 59.

5. Have students sort the cards into two groups: one group that sounds like words or phrases that could be associated with the main idea and one group that could be associated with details. Remind students that it can be difficult to know for certain whether a word or phrase will be used as a main idea or a detail.

6. Encourage students to predict how the words or phrases will be used as in the partial student example that follows.

Main Ideas	**Details**
Areas of land	Moist
Dark	Noisy
Rain forest	Birds

7. Ask students to explain why they identified words and phrases as main idea and details. As students discuss their rationales, help them understand how informational texts are organized as in the following example. You could also have students generate sample sentences using their words.

TEACHER: I see you have the words "rain forest," "areas of land," and "dark" as main ideas. Why did you choose those words and phrases?

STUDENT: I choose "rain forest" because it's the topic of the passage that we're reading. "Areas of land" is a pretty good definition for a land region and that's also what we're studying. I think rain forests are dark, so I choose that too.

> **TEACHER:** Good. Can you give me a sample first sentence using these words?
>
> **STUDENT:** Rain forests contain dark areas of land.
>
> **TEACHER:** That's pretty good. When you read, you'll find out whether you were close on that one.

8. After students read the passage, have them rearrange the word cards to fit the pattern of the passage. Remember that the pattern of informational text is difficult for all students so use this activity several times a month.

VARIATION

You can use Word Sort Cards for a variety of different purposes. For those students who need more opportunities to talk about a topic, for instance, you could create a group of cards about a theme and have students discuss the topic as they arrange the cards into the order of their speech. Have students who need to work on the order of the alphabet arrange the cards into alphabetical order. Word Sort Cards is a useful tool for many activities.

WORD SORT CARDS

During Reading Strategies

While students are reading, they should be actively trying to make meaning of the printed word. Constructing meaning is more challenging for students who are reading in a new language because they may be struggling with the kinds of language knowledge that native speakers unconsciously use. For example, when English-language learners are reading English texts, they may have difficulty with the linguistic components of English (Gass & Selinker, 2001). Therefore, teachers need frequently to model the uses of the cueing systems for students.

The cueing systems that readers use during reading are the semantic, syntactic, and grapho-phonetic language cues (Goodman, 1965). These cueing systems are also used when students read Spanish, but the linguistic rules that govern English are different. Native speakers of English are able to "hear" the syntactic cues, for example, because they have had wide exposure to the oral and written English language. Native English speakers know to place an adjective before a noun (e.g., a *blue* lamp) whereas in Spanish the adjective typically follows the noun, except in special circumstances (e.g., una lámpara *azul*). Spanish nouns, on the other hand, have an assigned gender, such as the masculine noun *el cielo* (the sun) or the feminine noun *la luna* (the moon). Since linguistic rules are different in Spanish and English, students who are learning to read in a new language cannot rely on how the language sounds until they become familiar with that language. The use of the cueing systems in one language, however, does seem to transfer to a second language (Bear, Templeton, Helman, & Baren, 2003). Teachers, therefore, need to help students learn to use the cueing systems appropriate for the language they are learning.

Good readers also monitor their comprehension as they read. Monitoring can take many forms, but it generally allows the reader to know when the text makes sense and when comprehension is breaking down. Good readers also know which strategies to use to repair the difficulty and to transcend the comprehension barrier. Teachers can instruct students in ways to monitor reading, but since monitoring is a cognitive process, it can be difficult to explain. Demonstrating comprehension-monitoring strategies through a think-aloud process tends to work best with native English speakers and with English-language learners (Peregoy & Boyle, 2001).

Readers who are able to monitor their comprehension during reading should also begin to question the text. Good readers ask questions of the text while reading, at times merely by exclaiming, "No way! This isn't right. What was the author thinking?" Readers who are active participants in reading events think during reading and this thinking can become questioning.

In addition to the types of questions that readers tend to think up during reading, readers should also consciously try to read critically and ask questions of the text. Critical literacy theories suggest that reading can be an avenue for actions leading to social justice. When students question the authority of texts and acknowledge the power of their own beliefs, they can use texts as a springboard for their own views. Critical literacy, therefore, has come to mean using texts to understand the social realities of the world and to actively contribute to changing cultures and furthering social justice (Kempe, 2001). Spanish-speaking students who are learning to read English should become aware of the power of the printed word and should learn to question biases

Sofia is thinking about the meaning of the text during reading.

that could be present in texts. Native speakers of English should also learn to question texts in Spanish because bias could also be present in Spanish language materials. The process of teaching questioning to students who are learning to read in a new language can open new ways of thinking for many students.

Teaching students to become strategic readers during reading is one of a teacher's most challenging goals. The strategies in this chapter are designed to teach students how to use the cueing systems, monitor reading, and question texts. When the strategies in this chapter are used with the other strategies in this book, students can become aware of a bevy of strategies that they can use to become strategic readers.

KIDPROJ'S Multicultural Calendar
www.kidlink.org/KIDPROJ/MCC
This online calendar of world cultural events, particularly holidays, has been compiled by learners—not all of them children, despite the site's name. The site welcomes submissions of new holidays from learners.

Aspectos Culturales
www.aspectosculturales.com
Shares aspects of Hispanic cultures with tapes, books, CDs, games, and much more.

SECTION 3.1   Accessing Cueing Systems

Instructional Goal: **To teach students to apply the cueing systems to figure out unknown words**

BACKGROUND

Reading is a complex undertaking, one that calls for strategic thinking during reading. When students read, they need to use the cues available to them to figure out words, and then they need to use those words to construct meaning. Reading, or decoding, words is much more than merely "sounding out words." In his seminal study on decoding words, Goodman (1965) concluded that reading is a psycholinguistic guessing game, an interaction between a reader's thoughts and the printed page in which readers use the cueing systems of language to figure out words.

The cueing systems that readers use to read English words are the phonological system, the syntactic system, and the semantic system or in other words

What cueing system do you think this teacher is showing students?

phonics, grammar, and word meaning. English, unlike Spanish, is not a phonetic language, which means that the letter/sound correlation in English is not a one-to-one match. In English, for example, the "long e" sound can be spelled 16 different ways: see, team, equal, he, key, Caesar, deceive, receipt, people, demesne, machine, field, debris, amoeba, quay, and pity (May, 1990). Readers of English, therefore, need to closely attend to the other cueing systems, such as the meaning cueing system and grammar. When students read English, they should try to understand the sounds of the letters and also check to see if the word they have read makes sense in the sentence. Using cueing systems in English is difficult for nonnative speakers because they are also learning the grammar of English and word meaning. Further, students learning a new language may overgeneralize the rules that they learn (Ariza, Morales-Jones, Yahya, & Zainuddin, 2002). When this occurs, teachers should be patient and continue teaching the cueing systems. Over time, students will learn when to apply different linguistic rules.

Students learning Spanish can also use the three cueing systems. Spanish is a phonetic language so when students are learning Spanish as a heritage language, they can apply their knowledge of the sound-symbol relationship to figure out new words. Students learning to read in Spanish should also be taught that when they read they should use the grammar of Spanish and word meaning in Spanish to figure out new words.

Center for Applied Linguistics
  www.cal.org
Provides topics in areas such as ESL literacy, bilingual education, K-12 ESL education, and many other resources for teachers to use.

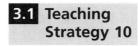

Word Strategy Bookmarks

When students read, they should use the cueing systems to figure out unknown words. The cueing systems that readers of English should use are phonics, grammar, and word meaning. When readers come to an unknown word, they should apply these cues flexibly, based on the need at the time. Teachers should instruct students on word-solving strategies, but students tend to "forget" these strategies as they read independently. Therefore, Johns, Lenski, and Berglund (2003) suggested that novice readers use a Word Strategy Bookmark to prompt them to use the cueing systems during reading.

DIRECTIONS AND EXAMPLES

1. Ask students what they do when they come to an unknown word when they are reading. If you are teaching students to read English, have students respond in English with ideas for reading English. If your language of instruction is Spanish, have students respond in Spanish about the strategies they use in Spanish. If you are teaching in a dual language classroom, you might have students respond in both languages and compare the strategies students use in each language. For example, you might suggest that some students "ask a neighbor" to tell them the word. Write the strategies that students use on the board. An example of one teacher's list for strategies in English follows.

Word-Solving Strategies We Use

  Ask a neighbor
  Ask the teacher
  Sound out the word
  Look at the picture

2. Tell students that many of the strategies they already use really help them figure out unknown words. Explain to students that there are other strategies they could use when they come to a word they don't know. Add these strategies to the list of Word-Solving Strategies as in the following example.

Word-Solving Strategies We Use

  Ask a neighbor
  Ask the teacher
  Sound out the word
  Look at the picture

More Strategies We Could Use

Try the beginning sound
Look for a familiar word part
Read on and come back to the word
Put in a word that makes sense

3. Select a piece of children's literature such as the bilingual book *Grandma and Me at the Flea: Los meros meros remateros* (Herrera, 2002) to demonstrate word-solving strategies. This book was written by Juan Felipe Herrera who is one of the most important Mexican-American poets. The illustrator is Anita de Lucio-Brock, a Mexican-born artist living in San Francisco. *Grandma and Me at the Flea: Los meros meros remateros* is a narrative poem written in Spanish, a story in poem form. The story rhymes in Spanish but not in English. Tell students that you will be demonstrating the word-solving strategies using this book. As you instruct students use the English version of the story if your language of instruction is English and use the Spanish version if you are teaching in Spanish.

4. Select one of the strategies to demonstrate for students. For example, if you wanted to use the strategy "Try the beginning sound," you would say something like the words that follow.

> When I read, sometimes I come across words that I don't know in English. I was reading the book *Grandma and Me at the Flea: Los meros meros remateros* yesterday, and I came across some words that I didn't know. I'll write the sentence on the board for you and leave blanks for the words that I didn't know.
>
> *"I smell _____ hot chocolate and my favorite- _____ eggs with* nopalitos, *juicy _____."*
>
> As I read the sentence I thought I'd try the beginning sound to try to figure out the words in the sentence. The first word began with a "t." The second letter was "o." I started saying the first two sounds to try to figure out the word.

5. Explain to students that "sounding out words" by trying the beginning sounds doesn't always work, especially in English. Remind students that English is not a phonetic language like Spanish is and that in English many sounds can be spelled with the same letters. Tell students that they should always try the beginning sound but that they need additional strategies to figure out unknown words.

6. Demonstrate a second strategy for students such as the strategy "look for word parts that you know." Remind students that many words in English have the same cognates as words in Spanish and that finding familiar word parts can help them figure out words in some cases. In other cases, students should not think about the Spanish cognates that they know but should try to think of English words that they know as in the example that follows.

"I smell _____ (toasty) _____ hot chocolate and my favorite _____ (scrambled) _____ eggs with nopalitos, juicy _____ (cactus) _____."

> I couldn't figure out the word by trying the beginning sounds so I looked at the entire word. The word is "toasty." I saw an English word that I knew, "toast," so I tried that and just added the ending sound. I figured out the first word using two strategies: "Try the beginning sound" and "Look for word parts that you know."

7. Demonstrate additional reading strategies during subsequent reading sessions. Examples of ways in which you could demonstrate the strategies using the same passage follow.

> When I came to the second blank, I tried a different strategy. I decided to "Read on and come back to the word." I tried the beginning sound, which in this case was "sc," but I still couldn't figure it out. So I read the rest of the sentence, and when I did, I could figure out that the word was "scrambled."

> For the last word, I tried another strategy because I couldn't figure out the word. The word "cactus" didn't have any familiar word parts and the word was at the end of the sentence so I couldn't read on. Instead, I decided to look at the pictures. However, I didn't see anything that represented the word in question. Then I tried to put in a word that makes sense until I could ask someone for help. I read the entire sentence again and thought about what I would add to scrambled eggs. I thought of chilies but I knew this word wasn't correct because I know how to spell "chilies." So I put in the word "chilies" until I could ask my friend who told me the word was "cactus." Then I read the entire sentence again.

8. Emphasize to students that when they come to a word that they cannot read they need to think about the word and figure it out using the strategies that they remember. Tell students that to help them remember word-solving strategies you have a Strategy Bookmark for them.

9. Duplicate and distribute one of the Strategy Bookmarks on pages 69–70. Use the English version if you are teaching the class in English and the Spanish version if you are teaching the class in Spanish. Duplicate several copies for students so that they can use them in each of the books they are reading.

10. Read each of the strategies on the bookmark and remind students that they should use one or more of these strategies when they come to an unfamiliar word. Continue demonstrating how to use these strategies throughout the year or until students use them independently.

ASSESSMENT IDEA

You can assess students' use of reading strategies by listening to them partner read with a friend. As students are reading, listen to the "helper partner" by noticing how the helper gives assistance to the reader. If the helper prompts the reader with the strategies you've taught, you can safely assume that the student has at least a working knowledge of word-solving strategies. If the helper does not suggest word-solving strategies but only says "Sound it out," you need to continue to demonstrate how students can use strategies to figure out unknown words.

STRATEGY BOOKMARK

1. Look at the pictures.

2. Get your mouth ready for the beginning sound.

3. Read on and come back to the word.

4. Put in a word that would make sense.

5. Look for the little parts that I know.

   CANDY

   C-AND-Y

6. Ask someone for help.

STRATEGY BOOKMARK

1. Mira las imágenes.

2. Prueba con el primer sonido.

3. Lee y regresa a la palabra.

4. Escribe una palabra que tenga sentido.

5. Busca las palabras que conoces.

   AMIGO
   A-MI-GO

6. Pide ayuda a alguien.

Using Picture Clues

When students are learning a new language, they need to access a variety of different types of clues to construct meaning from the story. Using Picture Clues is an additional strategy that students can use to help them understand what they are reading. Many picture books contain colorful pictures in them that can assist novice readers' reading comprehension. Not all students, however, have had experiences with picture books. Meier (2003) found that picture books were unfamiliar to many of her students. Some of these students were from immigrant backgrounds with financial struggles. The parents of these children did not have the resources to purchase books for their families. Furthermore, many parents, especially those from Latin America, have not experienced picture books themselves, so they may be unaware of the richness of children's literature. As a result of few experiences with picture books, some students will not know to use the pictures in books to help them figure out words' meanings. Using Picture Clues, however, can be taught to students learning both English and Spanish.

DIRECTIONS AND EXAMPLES

1. Select a book to demonstrate the strategy Using Picture Clues. Choose a book written in English if you are instructing the class in English or choose a book in Spanish if you are teaching in Spanish. Make sure the book you have chosen has pictures that can help students figure out unknown words. An excellent example of a picture book that is written in both languages is the English book *The Napping House* (Wood, 1984) or the Spanish version *La casa adormecida* (Wood 1985).

2. Duplicate and distribute one of the Using Picture Clues reproducibles on pages 75–76. Use the English version if you are teaching the class in English and use the Spanish version if you are teaching the class in Spanish.

3. Show the front cover of *The Napping House* to students and ask students what they think the title of the book means. Point out that in the picture the woman is sleeping on a bed with a young boy and a dog. Ask students what they think the people are doing. Then read the title of the book. Invite students to discuss how the picture on the cover relates to the title of the book.

4. Have students volunteer ways in which they can use the cover picture to figure out the title and to make predictions about the story. After the students have generated several ideas, have the students fill out their Using Picture Clues reproducibles. You might need to model what to write as in the following example.

Part of the Book	Picture Clues
Cover of the book	*I see a picture of a woman sleeping on a bed with a boy and a dog on top of her. The picture is funny so I think the book will also be funny. As I tried to figure out the words in the title, I tried to think of a word that means "to sleep" that begins with an "n." I figured out the title was* The Napping House.

Parte del Libro	Pistas de los Dibujos
Cubierta del libro	*Veo a una mujer durmiendo en una cama con un niño y un perro encima de ella. El dibujo es gracioso así que pienso que el libro también será divertido. Mientras trataba de entender las palabras en el título, traté de pensar en una palabra que signifique "dormir" que comience con una "a". Entonces comprendí que el título era* La casa adormecida.

5. Turn to the first page of the book and have students read the words and look at the picture. The first picture is of a house. If students have difficulty reading the words on the first page, have them look at the picture and see if the picture can help them figure out what the words are saying. Model the strategy Using Picture Clues as in the following example.

TEACHER: Sometimes when you read, you'll be able to use pictures to figure out the words on the page and what is happening in the story. Sometimes, however, the picture will not help you. Let's look at the first page and see in what ways the picture can help us. What do you see in the first picture?

STUDENT: A picture of a house.

TEACHER: Yes, read the words and see if the picture helps you with any of the words that you don't know. If you don't know a word, just say "blank."

STUDENT: "There is a house, a [blank] house where everyone is sleeping."

TEACHER: Let's look at the picture. Does it help you know what kind of house it is?

STUDENT: Not really.

TEACHER: Let's think back about the title. Does that help you?

STUDENT: Right, it's a napping house.

TEACHER: Correct. In this case the picture didn't help you but the title did. As you read, you need to use lots of different clues to help you figure out the words.

6. Read a few pages with students. After a few pages, show students how they can use picture clues to figure out words as in the following example.

TEACHER: What do you see in the pictures on this page?

STUDENT: I see an older woman, a boy, a cat, and a dog.

TEACHER: Good. Now, let's read the words on the page to see if the pictures can help us figure out the words.

STUDENT: [Reads the words on the page missing the word "granny."]

TEACHER:	You got almost all of the words. Let's try to figure out the word after snoring. Looking at the picture, you can see that's it's an older woman. What words can you use for an older woman?
STUDENT:	Grandmother, grandma.
TEACHER:	Yes, you can think of words that are close to the words on the page by using the picture. Now, let's look more closely at the letters in the words. Use other word-solving strategies to figure out the word.
STUDENT:	"Granny."
TEACHER:	Yes, notice how you used the picture clues with other reading strategies to figure out that word. Picture clues can really help you understand what you're reading.

7. After your demonstration, have students complete another row on the Using Picture Clues reproducibles. Model an example like the following one.

Part of the Book	Picture Clues
Cover of the book	I see a picture of a woman sleeping on a bed with a boy and a dog on top of her. The picture is funny so I think the book will also be funny. As I tried to figure out the words in the title, I tried to think of a word that means "to sleep" that begins with an "n." I figured out the title was The Napping House.
Page 10	I had trouble with the word "granny," but I used the picture with the sounds of the letters to figure it out.

Parte del Libro	Pistas de los Dibujos
Cubierta del libro	Veo a una mujer durmiendo en una cama con un niño y un perro encima de ella. El dibujo es gracioso así que pienso que el libro también será divertido. Mientras trataba de entender las palabras en el título, traté de pensar en una palabra que signifique "dormir" que comience con una "a". Entonces comprendí que el título era La casa adormecida.
Página 10	Tuve dificultad con la palaba "abuelita", pero usé el dibujo con los sonidos de las letras para entender la palabra.

8. Demonstrate how students can use picture clues as they read to figure out words and to understand the story until students can use the strategy independently. Have students use the reproducible Using Picture Clues occasionally so that they can learn how to think about pictures during reading.

VARIATION

Students can use picture clues in places other than picture books. Many of the signs and symbols in neighborhoods and public buildings contain pictures that students can decipher to make meaning. Provide an example of a sign that uses a picture to convey meaning, such as a "Slippery when Wet!" sign. Show students how the pictures and words are used to make the message clear. Many signs are in both English and Spanish and, if this is the case, point out the messages in both languages.

NAME _____ DATE _____

USING PICTURE CLUES

Book Title _____

Author _____

Part of Book	Picture Clues

NOMBRE _____ FECHA _____

USING PICTURE CLUES

Título _____

Autor _____

Parte del Libro	Pistas de los Dibujos

Fix-Up Strategies

Once students have learned how to use the cueing systems to figure out unknown words, they need to monitor their use of the strategies during reading. Teaching the cueing systems to students is difficult, but far more difficult is having students use these strategies independently. Research indicates, however, that good readers not only flexibly use reading strategies but also monitor the use of the strategies they've used (Pressley, 1995). Having students use reading strategies when they are learning to read a new language is even more complex. In fact, Ariza, Morales-Jones, Yahya, and Zainuddin (2002) state that teachers are better able to help second-language learners "if they understand a myriad of effective strategies and apply them in their teaching techniques and materials" (p. 204). By having teachers frequently demonstrate strategies and having students monitor their use of strategies, students can learn to flexibly use strategies during reading.

All readers have times when their reading breaks down and they need to apply "fix-up" strategies. Good readers, however, monitor their comprehension and are able to quickly apply the necessary strategies so that they can continue reading without delay. Many students do not use fix-up strategies consciously, so teachers need to help them understand what to do when they run into difficulty reading a particular text.

DIRECTIONS AND EXAMPLES

1. Tell students that when they read they should think about whether or not the words make sense and whether they understand what they have read. Explain to students that good readers use cueing systems during reading, use picture clues, and monitor their own progress. Remind students that sometimes readers have difficulty but that good readers apply fix-up strategies during reading.

2. Since many students will not have heard the term "fix-up strategies," explain the term to students using something like the following example.

> When you read, sometimes you don't know the words and you don't know what's happening. You need to "fix" your reading because it's not working. "Fix" is a word that means to "repair" or to "mend." You may have heard someone say, "My car is broken. I need to get it fixed." Just like you can fix a broken car, you can also "fix" your reading when you get stuck. Today we're going to talk about ways to apply fix-up strategies.

3. Duplicate and distribute one of the reproducibles on pages 79-80. If you are teaching in English, use the English reproducible, or if you are teaching in Spanish, use the Spanish reproducible.

4. Read the chart headings with students. Explain what each one means by saying something like the following comments.

> Let's look at the chart called Fix-Up Strategies. The first column has the words "Identify Problem." That means to write down things that don't make sense to you. This is where your reading is having trouble and needs to get "fixed."

The next four columns are examples of Fix-Up Strategies that good readers use. They are "Look Back and Reread," "Read Ahead," "Ask Questions," and "Solve Unknown Words." These are things you can do to fix your reading when you have difficulty. You can use this chart to help you keep track of the Fix-Up Strategies that you use.

5. Select a book that you can use to demonstrate the strategy Fix-Up Strategies or use the bilingual book *This House is Made of Mud: Esta casa está hecha de lodo* (Buchman, 1991). Use the English version if you are teaching the class in English or use the Spanish version if you are teaching the class in Spanish.

6. Read parts of the book with students. Pretend you are having trouble reading and need to use a fix-up strategy as in the following example.

> I was reading the book *This House is Made of Mud* when I ran into difficulty. I read how the house was built and that insects and mice live in the house. Then the book said that the house has a yard called the desert. I read the word "dessert" like the sweets you eat after a meal. It didn't make sense to me so I wrote that in my chart under "Identify Problem."
>
> I decided to use the fix-up strategy "Look Back and Reread." I reread from the beginning of the story but it still didn't make sense. I'll write in my chart that rereading didn't help.
>
> Then I decided to think about whether I had read all of the words accurately. I looked at the word "desert" and remembered that the English words "desert" and "dessert" look very much alike. I tried solving the word by changing the word to "desert." Then the story made sense. I then added that to my chart.

FIX-UP STRATEGIES				
Identify Problem	**Look Back and Reread**	**Read Ahead**	**Ask Questions**	**Solve Unknown Words**
I wondered how the house could have a "dessert" around it. That doesn't make sense.	*Reread from the beginning but it didn't help.*			*Remembered that "desert" and "dessert" are similar in in English. Changed words and it made sense.*

7. Continue reading the book until you come to other sections where you could demonstrate using Fix-Up Strategies during reading. Demonstrate using Fix-Up Strategies frequently until students are able to use the chart independently.

NAME _____ DATE _____

FIX-UP STRATEGIES

Identify Problem	Look Back and Reread	Read Ahead	Ask Questions	Solve Unknown Words

NOMBRE _____ FECHA _____

FIX-UP STRATEGIES

Identificar Problema	Retroceder y Leer de Nuevo	Adelantarse en la Lectura	Hacer Preguntas	Adivinar Palabras Desconocidas

SECTION 3.2 # Monitoring Understanding

> *Instructional Goal:* **To help students learn how to monitor their understanding of what they read**

BACKGROUND

When students read, they need to monitor their understanding of text. Research indicates that good readers monitor their comprehension during reading while struggling readers do not (Paris & Jacobs, 1984). Some of the strategies that good readers use are making predictions and connections during reading. When

students monitor the predictions and/or connections they make, they are able to learn more about their individual reading processes and consciously use these strategies when they are faced with new texts. Students who are learning either English or Spanish benefit from instruction in metacognitive and cognitive strategies. In fact, García (2003) points out that students who are taught monitoring strategies in their heritage language can apply these strategies to their new language. This means that teachers should teach students to make predictions and connections when they read both in English and in Spanish.

How does Carlos monitor his comprehension?

Teaching students how to monitor their comprehension is difficult. Many students don't know what strategies good readers use. Therefore, it's important that teachers help students think about how good readers approach text before they begin teaching monitoring strategies.

National Clearinghouse for English Language Acquisition and Language Instruction Educational Programs
www.ncela.gwu.edu

This Department of Education website offers practical resources for linguistically and culturally diverse classrooms.

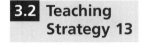

3.2 Teaching Strategy 13

What Good Readers Do

One way to help students discuss the strategies good readers use is through image-based discussion of reading strategies (Cobb, 2003). Before students can really understand how to monitor their reading, they need to think about what good readers do. Although there are surveys to give students to rate their metacognitive awareness, Cobb (2003) suggests that teachers use pictures of children and adults reading to begin discussions about what good readers do as they read. This discussion, then, can help students begin to understand the reading process, and through teacher scaffolding, students can increase their awareness of metacognitive strategies to monitor their reading.

DIRECTIONS AND EXAMPLES

1. Tell students that good readers use a variety of strategies to make sense of their reading. Explain that good readers can be children or adults, that age doesn't dictate whether a person will be an effective reader.

2. Ask students to think about people they know who are good readers. Divide the class into groups of three or four students and have students develop a list of people they know who are good readers. Tell students that many of their classmates are good readers but not to select anyone from the class for this list. After students are finished talking, compile a list as in the example that follows.

Good Readers I Know

My father
My teacher
Uncle Diego
Juan
Carlos
Jeremy
Patricia
Amy
Maria

3. Tell students that all of them can also be good readers but they need to think about what good readers do.

4. Duplicate and distribute one of the What Good Readers Do reproducibles on pages 84–85. If you are instructing students in English, use the English version, or if you are instructing students in Spanish, use the Spanish version.

5. Place a variety of photos of children and adults reading in a place for students to see or use the photographs that follow on page 83. Try to have a variety of ethnic groups represented in the pictures. The pictures should provide students with a mental image of reading as they discuss the characteristics of good readers.

6. Tell students that many different people are good readers and that all good readers have some common strategies that they use.

7. Have students look at the pictures and answer the questions on the reproducible What Good Readers Do.

8. After students have answered the questions independently, divide the class into groups of three or four students and have them discuss their ideas.

9. Discuss the questions as an entire class. Emphasize that good readers use strategies such as word solving, predicting, and connecting. Encourage students to use these strategies so that they become good readers.

ASSESSMENT IDEA

Repeat this strategy after several months to determine whether students are learning how to become good readers. If they don't know what good readers do, spend time discussing ways in which readers use reading strategies before, during, and after reading. Keep a list of the strategies that you teach so that students can refer to the strategies as they read.

PHOTOGRAPHS OF READERS

From Susan Davis Lenski and Fabiola Ehlers-Zavala, *Reading Strategies for Spanish Speakers.* Copyright © 2004 by Kendall/Hunt Publishing Company (1-800-247-3458). May be reproduced for noncommercial educational purposes.

NAME _____ DATE _____

WHAT GOOD READERS DO

1. What is the reader in the photograph doing to be a good reader?

   _____

   _____

   _____

2. What do you suppose the reader is thinking as he or she reads?

   _____

   _____

   _____

3. What strategies do you think this reader is using?

   _____

   _____

   _____

4. What makes a good reader?

   _____

   _____

   _____

5. Are you a good reader? Why or why not?

   _____

   _____

   _____

NOMBRE _____ FECHA _____

WHAT GOOD READERS DO

1. ¿Qué está haciendo el lector o lectora en la fotografía para ser un buen lector?

_____

_____

_____

2. ¿Qué crees que el lector o lectora está pensando mientras él o ella lee?

_____

_____

_____

3. ¿Qué estrategias crees que este lector o lectora está usando?

_____

_____

_____

4. ¿Qué hace a un buen lector o lectora?

_____

_____

_____

5. ¿Eres tú un buen lector o una buena lectora? ¿Por qué sí o por qué no?

_____

_____

_____

3.2 Teaching Strategy 14

Prediction Chart

Making and confirming predictions is an important part of reading. When successful students read texts, they make predictions before they read and during reading. As with most reading strategies, predicting is done very quickly, almost at a subconscious level. As they read, readers are constantly thinking, "I wonder what will happen next?"

Students who are learning to read, however, may not be as engaged in the reading process as good readers are, and they may not make predictions while reading. Since making prediction helps readers stay involved in the story, offering students an organizational structure for their predictions, such as a Prediction Chart, can help them learn to use predictions on an ongoing basis.

When teachers demonstrate and model the use of a Prediction Chart, students who do not predict during reading can understand how prediction can be used. Frequent demonstrations of strategies are especially important for students who are learning a new language. As with other content, reading strategies need to be made accessible to students. As Hernández (2003) states, "Teachers must provide students with modeling of the strategies needed to comprehend content material and content instruction" (p. 131). Making predictions is one of the key strategies in reading comprehension; therefore, teachers need to take the time to frequently model predictions with their students.

DIRECTIONS AND EXAMPLES

1. Tell students that while reading they should make predictions about the story. Define the word "prediction" so that students understand what you mean, by saying something like the words that follow.

   Making a prediction while reading is like guessing what will happen next. For example, when you watch a movie, you probably guess what will happen, even if you don't say anything and just think about it. The brain constantly makes predictions for you. When you read, you should keep your mind actively involved in the story by making predictions.

2. Demonstrate how to make predictions with a story that is unfamiliar to students. If you are teaching the class in English, for example, you might choose *Abuela's Weave* (Castañeda, 1993a), or if you are teaching the class in Spanish you might choose the Spanish version, *El tapiz de abuela* (Castañeda, 1993b). *Abeuela's Weave* was written by Omar S. Castañeda, who was born in Guatemala, and was illustrated by Enrique O. Sanchez, an artist born in the Dominican Republic.

3. Duplicate and distribute one of the Prediction Charts on pages 90–91. Use the English reproducible if you are teaching the class in English or use the Spanish reproducible if you are teaching the class in Spanish.

4. Divide the class into groups of three or four students. Make sure one of the students in each group is proficient in the language of instruction. Read the title of the book with the students and ask them to look at the cover of the book. Ask them to predict, or guess, what the story will be

about. Provide students with an example of a prediction similar to the one that follows.

> When I see the cover of this book and look at the picture, I notice that the houses and people do not look like people living in the United States. Since I know that the author is from Guatemala, I'm guessing that the story takes place there rather than in the United States. I also see an older woman and a young girl with a hand loom, so I'm guessing that the story will be about a grandmother who is teaching her granddaughter how to weave a blanket.

5. Provide each group of students with time to make predictions about the story in their groups. Have students write their predictions on the Prediction Chart as in the example that follows.

Part of Book	My Prediction	Was I Right? Why or Why Not?
Title and Cover	*Grandmother teaching granddaughter how to weave*	

Parte del Libro	Mi Predicción	¿Tuve Razón? ¿Por Qué o Por Qué No?
Título y portada	*Abuela enseñando a tejer a su nieta*	

6. Tell students that they will "confirm" their predictions, or determine whether they were accurate, when they begin reading the story.
7. Read the story with students or have students read it independently. Stop after a few pages to have students confirm their original predictions and to make additional predictions. Demonstrate what you mean by instructing students as follows.

> I began reading the book and I discovered that my original prediction was accurate. *Abuela's Weave* is about a grandmother who is teaching her granddaughter, Esperanza, to weave. As I read further, however, I found out that there was more to the story. I found out that Esperanza was ashamed of her grandmother because of a birthmark and worried that no one would buy their weavings.
>
> Abuela and Esperanza are going to a market to sell their weavings. Esperanza is worried. I predict that Esperanza will not sell anything and that they'll go back to their village crying.

8. Have students write their predictions and how accurate they were about their first predictions on the Prediction Chart as in the example that follows.

Part of Book	My Prediction	Was I Right? Why or Why Not?
Title and Cover	Grandmother teaching granddaughter how to weave	Yes, I was right. The story is about a grandmother teaching Esperanza how to weave.
First half of book	Grandmother and Esperanza will take their blankets to the market and not sell anything. They'll go home crying.	

Parte del Libro	Mi Predicción	¿Tuve Razón? ¿Por Qué o Por Qué No?
Título y portada	Abuela enseñando a tejer a su nieta	Sí, tuve razón. La historia se trata de una abuela enseñando a tejer a Esperanza.
Primera mitad del libro	La abuela y Esperanza van a llevar sus mantas al mercado y no van a vender nada. Van a regresar a casa llorando.	

9. Have students read the remaining half of the book, making predictions, writing them on their Prediction Charts, and confirming their predictions.

10. Model the prediction strategy several times until the students feel confident that they can predict independently. Have students use the Prediction Chart frequently but not for every story that they read. Tell students that they need to make predictions by themselves when they read without the Prediction Chart. Remind students that the Prediction Chart is a tool to help them remember to make predictions during reading but that they should make predictions all of the time, not just when they are using the Prediction Chart.

VARIATION

Have students make predictions during other types of learning activities. For example, when students are adding numbers in mathematics, have students make a "prediction," or a guess, before determining the correct answer. Explain to students that they make predictions in many other aspects of life as well. Encourage students to discuss the types of predictions they make. Draw parallels between the students' answers and making predictions during reading.

NAME _____ DATE _____

PREDICTION CHART

Part of Book	My Prediction	Was I Right? Why or Why Not?

NOMBRE _____ FECHA _____

PREDICTION CHART

Parte del Libro	Mi Predicción	¿Tuve Razón? ¿Por Qué o Por Qué No?

From Susan Davis Lenski and Fabiola Ehlers-Zavala, *Reading Strategies for Spanish Speakers*. Copyright © 2004 by Kendall/Hunt Publishing Company (1-800-247-3458). May be reproduced for noncommercial educational purposes.

3.2 Teaching Strategy 15

Connections Chart

In order for students to construct rich, personal meanings from text, they should make connections to their own experiences and to their lives. However, many students do not think about how school texts relate to their lives without the teacher's intervention (Hartman, 1995). One way to help students make connections is through the use of a Connections Chart (Johns & Lenski, 2001). Connections Charts help students think about the texts as they read, connect them to their lives, and also make connections to school learning. According to Lenski (2001), students can learn to make connections to other school subjects when teachers demonstrate connecting activities. The Connections Chart is one way for students to make connections to their lives and to school learning.

Connections Charts are a valuable tool for helping students who are learning a new language to think about ways in which the book they are reading relates to their culture. Colombi and Roca (2003) remind us to "take into account the attitudinal and sociohistorical factors affecting students in the environment in which we teach" (p. 4). When students are able to connect their current learning with their personal lives outside school and in school, they begin to see the relevancy of the books they are reading, which can help students become more engaged in their learning.

DIRECTIONS AND EXAMPLES

1. Tell students that when they read they should make connections to their lives, other books they have read, and things they've learned in school. Explain to students that they probably already think about their own experiences as they read. Provide an example of a book you've read and things that came to mind as in the example that follows.

    > Last night I finished reading the book *Flight to Freedom* by Ana Veciana-Suarez (2002) which was a book about a girl names Yara and how her family came to the United States from Cuba. I thought about how my grandmother came to the United States from Mexico when she was a girl and how afraid she was. The book also reminded me of another book we read in this class, *My diary from Here to There: Mi Diario de Aqúi hasta Allá* (Pérez, 2002), about another young girl who emigrated from Mexico. I also thought about our geography lesson when we were learning about the Spanish-speaking countries. One of the countries we studied was Cuba. As I read *Flight to Freedom,* then, I made all sorts of connections—some were to my life, some were to books I have read, and some were to things I've learned in school.

2. Tell students that when they hear stories or read they should also try to make connections. Explain that they can use a Connections Chart to remind them to make connections when they read. Explain to students that when they make connections they are able to understand the text better.

3. Demonstrate the Connections Chart by selecting a story or a passage with which students are unfamiliar. Select a story in English if you are instructing students in English or select a story in Spanish if you are instructing them in Spanish. You might want to demonstrate Connections Charts with either the English version, *Hey, Little Ant* (Hoose & Hoose, 1998a), or the Spanish version, *Oye, hormiguita* (Hoose & Hoose, 1998b).

4. Duplicate and distribute one of the Connections Charts on pages 96–97. Use the English version if you are teaching in English or the Spanish version if you are teaching students in Spanish. Give each student a copy of the Connections Chart.

5. Show students the title of the story and ask students what they think the story will be about. For example, if you are using the story *Hey, Little Ant*, a conversation might be as follows.

TEACHER:	Write the title of the story on the top of our Connections Chart. Then look at the front cover and think about the title. What do you think this story will be about?
ELENA:	The picture shows a little ant looking at a boy's glasses. The ant looks scared. Maybe the story will be about a boy and his pet ant.
TEACHER:	That's a wonderful prediction. What do you think about when you see the cover and hear the title? Try to make connections to your lives, books you've read, and things you've learned in school.
PAULO:	I think about our science book when we studied insects.
JUAN:	I think about the ants that live in our sidewalk. We have thousands of ants.
ELIZABETH:	I think about fire ants that I heard about from my sister who lives in Texas.
MAYRA:	I think about all of the ants that came to our picnic last weekend.
TEACHER:	These are all wonderful connections. When you read, you need to make connections to help you understand the story.

6. Read the story to students or have them read the story in pairs. Stop halfway through the story and have students think about the connections they could make to the story. In *Hey, Little Ant*, a boy is ready to step on an ant that begins to plead for its life. The ant gives the boy reasons why he shouldn't kill it. The boy thinks of reasons why ants are insignificant to him or why they are pests.

7. Divide the class into groups of three or four students. Make sure a proficient speaker of the language of instruction is in each of the groups. Have students discuss the connections they could make to this story.

8. Have students discuss the connections they made with the entire class. Tell students that when one person makes a connection, that idea might trigger students to make additional connections.

9 Write the connections students made on a Connections Chart or have students write them independently. An example follows.

Story Title	Hey, Little Ant
Connections to other books	*Science book about insects* *Book from library on ants* *Books that show one person in power like* *Click, Clack, Moo: Cows that Type* *Two Bad Ants, a story I heard last year*
Connections to school learning	*Science unit: Insects* *Communities* *Discussion about bullies*
Connections to self	*Ants at a picnic* *Stepping on ants at home* *Fire ants* *Ants in our kitchen* *We had ants in our school in Mexico.*

Titulo	Oye, hormiguita

Conexiones con otros libros	*Libro de ciencia acerca de insectos*
	Libro de biblioteca sobre hormigas
	Libros que muestran una persona en poder
	    como, Clic, clac, muu: Vacas escritoras
	Dos hormigas malas, una historia que oí el año
	    pasado

Conexiones con el sabiduría en la esculela	*Unidad en ciencias: insectos* *Comunidades* *Discusión acerca de matones*
Conexiones con uno mismo	*Hormigas en un picnic* *Pisar hormigas en casa* *Hormigas en la cocina* *Nosotros teníamos hormigas en nuestra* *escuela en México.*

10. Demonstrate the Connections Chart several times using a variety of different books. As students become more proficient with making connections, encourage them to use the Connections Chart when they read independently. Have students make connections frequently so that they become accustomed to thinking about ways in which school learning is connected to other types of learning.

VARIATION

At times you may want to have students make connections to various subject content that you are teaching. If you want students to make direct connections, change the chart to include the topics you want students to use. For example, if you read a book about weather during reading class, you may want students to make connections to science, geography, and communities. List those topics on the chart for students to use as students make connections during reading.

NAME _____ DATE _____

CONNECTIONS CHART

Story Title	
Connections to other books	
Connections to school learning	
Connections to self	

NOMBRE _____ FECHA _____

CONNECTIONS CHART

Título	
Conexiones con otros libros	
Conexiones con el aprendizaje escolar	
Conexiones con uno mismo	

SECTION 3.3 | Questioning Text

Instructional Goal: **To encourage students to ask questions about text while they are reading**

BACKGROUND

All readers need to be active participants in reading events, especially students who are learning a new language. When students are reading a new language, they need to balance the need for understanding the vocabulary in the text with the text's message. Often a reader's concern for understanding new words takes precedence over constructing meaning, sometimes because English/Spanish language teachers emphasize learning words over comprehension. This overemphasis on knowing words is one of the reasons why students learning English score low on tests of comprehension and why Spanish-speaking students are kept from becoming proficient reading in their own language (see García & Beltrán, 2003; Lynch, 2003).

One way for all students to become more engaged in reading is to ask questions during reading. Good readers question, rapidly and silently, as they read; their minds are constantly working while reading. Some of the questions that readers ask are simply aids to recall parts of the text, but other questions come into the area of critical literacy.

Critical literacy is an evolving set of beliefs about reading texts that is based on Freire's idea that readers should read texts critically and then move beyond reading to become agents against oppression and for social justice. Readers should also be engaged in a critical analysis of the social framework in which they exist (Freire, 1985). Freire's works, along with those of other social learning theorists, have contributed to what we now call critical literacy (Green, 2001).

Critical literacy theories suggest that texts are products of social beings who have feelings, biases, and opinions (Wink, 2001). A critical reading of texts can uncover these biases, which, in turn, can lead to actions of social justice. A definition of critical literacy is "an active, challenging approach to literacy that encourages students to be aware of the way that texts are constructed and how such constructions position readers" (Fehring & Green, 2001, back cover). Readers recognize that texts are not neutral—texts influence and establish social identity and power relationships, and texts can reproduce or challenge cultural relationships (Luke, O'Brien, & Comber, 2001). When readers ask questions of texts, they not only become engaged readers, but they also enter into the reading situation with the power to agree or disagree with the author.

What questions can these students ask to deepen their comprehension?

Questioning that involves the principles of critical literacy can help students who are learning a new language to keep their personal integrity while reading.

Many Languages, Many Cultures
www.teacher.scholastic.com/professional/teachstrat/manylanguages.htm
Gives teachers suggestions and strategies to be able to teach as racial, cultural, and linguistic diversity increases.

Teaching for Change
www.teachingforchange.org
This organization's publications and videos are intended for K-12 classrooms, but many materials can be adapted to other settings. Click on the "catalog" link on the left-hand side of the page to obtain an extensive listing of books, videos, and posters for the K-12 classroom. Click on News for extensive resources about current events.

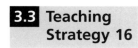

3.3 Teaching Strategy 16

Paired Questioning

When students read, they should be engaged in thinking about the text they are reading by constantly asking questions about the content of the text. This questioning is done at a subconscious level in many respects and occurs in very brief amounts of time (see RAND Reading Study Group, 2002). Students who struggle with reading, however, may not be thinking about the text as often as good readers are, and they may not be asking questions during reading. McLaughlin and Allen (2002) recommend that students ask each other questions using the strategy Paired Questioning to practice this cognitive process. When students become comfortable asking questions about reading, they have a greater likelihood of using the strategy independently.

DIRECTIONS AND EXAMPLES

1. Tell students that one way to become a good reader is to ask questions during reading. Explain to students that when you (as the teacher) read to yourself you ask questions all the time you're reading. Tell students that when you ask questions, you become more interested in your reading and are able to remember what you have read.

2. Demonstrate how to ask questions during reading by reading a book to students and asking questions that pertain to the story. For example, you might use the bilingual book *My Diary from Here to There: Mi diario de aquí hasta allá* (Pérez, 2002) to model the strategy. If you are teaching the class in English read the English version, and if you're teaching the class in Spanish, read the Spanish version. Ask the questions in the language of instruction.

3. Tell students about the book before reading. *My Diary from Here to There: Mi diario de aquí hasta allá* is a book written in diary form about the trip from Mexico to Los Angeles of the author, Amada Irma Pérez. Ask students if they are familiar with diaries. Explain to students that a diary is a book filled with entries, or letters, about the life of the author.

4. Read the book before the lesson and write down several questions you could ask while reading. Then read the first few pages of the book to students and ask them if they have any questions. If students do not have any questions, provide a few of your own. After demonstrating how to ask questions for the first few pages, read several more pages and ask more questions. Continue until you've read the entire book. Questions follow for *My Diary from Here to There: Mi diario de aquí hasta allá* in the sequence of the story. The first few questions could be asked after the first few pages and so on.

- ◆ Will the family really move to Los Angeles?
- ◆ Will Amada's friend Michi forget about her?
- ◆ Will their grandparents have room for their family to stay in Mexicali?
- ◆ Will Amada's father get a job?
- ◆ Will they all get green cards?
- ◆ Will they like Los Angeles?
- ◆ Will the family go back to Mexico?
- ◆ ¿Se mudará realmente la familia a Los Angeles?
- ◆ ¿Se olvidará Michi de Amada?
- ◆ ¿Tendrán espacio sus abuelos para su familia en Mexicali?
- ◆ ¿Conseguirá trabajo el papá de Amada?
- ◆ ¿Conseguirán todos la tarjeta de residencia?
- ◆ ¿Les gustará Los Angeles?
- ◆ ¿Regresará la familia a México?

5. Ask students whether they ask questions like these when they read. Explain to students that many people ask questions even when they aren't aware of it. Provide students with the opportunity to discuss how they feel about this strategy.

6. Tell students that they will be practicing this questioning strategy in groups of two and that the strategy is called Paired Questioning. Remind students that the word "pair" means two and that in Paired Questioning students will be in groups of two to ask each other questions about books they are reading.

7. Divide the class into groups of two. Try to match proficient language users with novice language users. Provide the pairs of students with books that they will be able to read independently.

8. Duplicate and distribute one of the Paired Questioning reproducibles on pages 102–103. Read the directions with students. Instruct students to read the first half of the book and then write down two or three questions. Help students if necessary.

9. Ask the pairs of students to ask each other their questions. Have one student ask his or her questions and the other one answer the questions. Then have the students switch roles.

10. Have students read the remaining portion of their books, ask and answer one student's questions, then switch roles.
11. After students have completed the Paired Questioning strategy, discuss ways in which the strategy was useful and ways in which students thought the strategy was not useful.
12. Provide guidance with Paired Questioning as many times as needed until students are able to work in pairs without your support. Remind students that they should be asking questions while reading even when they are not participating in the strategy in class.

VARIATION

Encourage students to ask different kinds of questions as they read. Raphael (1986) suggests that students ask four kinds of questions: Right There questions, or questions that have answers that can be found in the text; Think and Search questions, or questions that can be answered by making inferences about the text; Author and You questions, or questions whose answers are not in the text but are implied; and On My Own questions, or questions that relate to personal experience. Teach students to ask each kind of question and encourage them to vary their questions while reading.

NAME _____ DATE _____

PAIRED QUESTIONING

Directions: Read the first half of the book and write down two or three questions that you have about the story. Ask your partner the questions and listen to your partner's answers. Then read the rest of the book, write down questions, and ask them to your partner.

Questions about first half of book

1. _____
_____

2. _____
_____

3. _____
_____

Questions about second half of book

1. _____
_____

2. _____
_____

3. _____
_____

NOMBRE _____ FECHA _____

PAIRED QUESTIONING

Direcciones: Lee la primera mitad del libro y escribe dos o tres preguntas que tengas acerca de la historia. Haz las preguntas a tu compañero/a y escucha sus respuestas. Luego lee el resto del libro, escribe preguntas, y hazlas a tu compañero/a.

Preguntas acerca de la primera mitad del libro

1. _____
_____

2. _____
_____

3. _____
_____

Preguntas acerca de la segunda mitad del libro

1. _____
_____

2. _____
_____

3. _____
_____

Questioning the Author

When students read, they should think about themselves as readers who have the power to construct meaning. As students construct meaning, they need to visualize that authors are people like themselves who have written a story or a text. These texts are rarely "questioned" by readers but rather are often considered to be perfect. To combat this type of thinking, Beck, McKeown, Hamilton, and Kucan (1997) developed the Questioning the Author strategy to encourage readers to identify authors as real people who are trying to present a message, which may or may not have flaws. Questioning the Author is a strategy that was developed for older students reading nonfictional texts, but Johns, Lenski, and Berglund (2003) adapted the strategy for young students reading both fictional and informational texts.

Questioning the Author is a strategy that can also be used for students who are learning a new language. When Spanish-speaking students in North America are learning English, for example, teachers are encouraged to give students books with multicultural settings (e.g., Ada, 2003). Students who have had primary experience with the cultures represented in the stories, however, could have opinions about how well the authors wrote the stories. On the other hand, students in North America who are in programs where they are reading Spanish texts might find that many of their books have been translated from English. The students might question some of the ways in which the story is being told in Spanish. When students use the Questioning the Author strategy, they are given "permission" to find fault with the translation of the book or with the way the author told the story. This strategy, therefore, empowers students to become real co-constructors of the texts they read.

DIRECTIONS AND EXAMPLES

1. Select a book that was written either in English or in Spanish that you want to use to demonstrate the Questioning the Author strategy or use the bilingual book *El diente flojo, flojito, flojote: The Wibbly Wobbly Tooth* (Mills & Crouth, 2003). Read the book in English if you are teaching the class in English or read it in Spanish if Spanish is the language of instruction for the class.

2. Explain to students that authors do the best job they can to express their ideas but that sometimes authors aren't clear about what they're trying to say. Hold up the book you have chosen and say something like the following statements.

    > This book is titled *The Wibbly Wobbly Tooth* and it was written by two authors whose names are David Mills and Julia Crouth. These two authors have written a book about a loose tooth. Think about these two authors as I tell you a bit more about the book.

3. Read the short description of the book on the back cover. The book is written to celebrate the "diverse traditions associated with losing a baby tooth." Point out that this book has been translated into several languages. Explain

to students that many books have information about the books and/or the authors on the back covers. Tell students that this book does not give biographies of the authors.

4. Read the book to students or have students read the book independently.
5. Divide the class into groups of three or four students. Make sure that each group has a student who is proficient in the language of instruction. Ask students to share their experiences with loosing teeth. Encourage students to talk in the language of instruction.

6. Duplicate and distribute one of the Questioning the Author reproducibles on pages 106–107. Use the English version if you are instructing the class in English or use the Spanish version if you are instructing the class in Spanish. Read the questions with the students, making sure that all students understand the questions. Rephrase questions that students don't understand.
7. Ask students to apply some of the Questioning the Author questions to the book *El diente flojo, flojito, flojote: The Wibbly Wobbly Tooth.* Conduct a class discussion using the names of the authors in the questions. Modify the questions to follow the students' discussion. You don't need to have students ask all of the questions on the sheet. An example follows.

TEACHER:	What are David Mills and Julia Crouth trying to say in this book?
STUDENT:	They are telling us about a boy named Li who lost his tooth.
TEACHER:	Do you think Mills and Crouth told the story clearly?
STUDENT:	Well, it was pretty clear, but I don't think the author told us enough. I wish the story had more children in it and more ideas about what children do when they loose teeth.
TEACHER:	What would you put in the story?
STUDENT:	In my house, we put the tooth in a small plastic case and put the case on the table. I would add that.
TEACHER:	What else would you put in the story if you were the author?
STUDENT:	I would put something more about what Li did at school.
TEACHER:	It's good to think about what the author decided to do when writing the story and thinking about what you liked and didn't like.

8. Encourage students to use Questioning the Author when reading by posting the questions in a prominent place in the classroom. Direct students' attention to the questions whenever a situation occurs in which students could use this strategy.
9. Students will need many experiences using Questioning the Author in groups before they feel comfortable using this strategy independently.

NAME _____ DATE _____

QUESTIONING THE AUTHOR

1. What is the author trying to say in this book?

   _____

   _____

   _____

2. Did the author tell the story clearly?

   _____

   _____

   _____

3. Is the author good at writing for students my age? Why or why not?

   _____

   _____

   _____

4. What could the author have done to make the story easier to understand?

   _____

   _____

   _____

5. If the story is a translation, does it accurately portray conversation in English?

   _____

   _____

   _____

6. In what ways did the author do a good job?

   _____

   _____

   _____

NOMBRE _____ FECHA _____

QUESTIONING THE AUTHOR

1. ¿Qué está tratando de decir en este libro el autor?

   _____

   _____

   _____

2. ¿Contó el autor la historia claramente?

   _____

   _____

   _____

3. ¿Escribe el autor bien para estudiantes de mi edad? ¿Por qué o por qué no?

   _____

   _____

   _____

4. ¿Qué pudo haber hecho el autor para hacer la historia mas fácil de entender?

   _____

   _____

   _____

5. ¿Si la historia es una traducción, representa con precisión una conversación en inglés?

   _____

   _____

   _____

6. ¿De que manera realizó el autor un buen trabajo?

   _____

   _____

   _____

3.3 Teaching Strategy 18

Problematizing Text

During reading, students should blend their personal responses to texts with their critical thinking ability to acknowledge the "power of the text on the reader as well as an understanding of *why* the text exercises that power" (Soter, 1999, p. 114). To further this reading skill, students can problematize texts as they read (Comber, 2001). Students problematize texts by analyzing the specific words authors choose to create an emotion or to set a tone and by recognizing that all writers choose words, either consciously or unconsciously, to influence readers. Students should also recognize that texts are not neutral— they influence and establish social identity and power relationships (Luke, O'Brien, Comber, 2001). As students read, therefore, they should think about how texts can reproduce or challenge cultural relationships and look for the ways in which reality is constructed in texts by asking and answering questions as they read.

DIRECTIONS AND EXAMPLES

1. Select a text that has a rich enough story line to analyze. Most of the examples of children's literature used in this book are stories that could be used for the problematizing strategy.
2. Tell students that they will be questioning texts in a different way when they read. Remind students that they should be questioning as they read and that you will be demonstrating a different type of questioning.
3. Explain to students that texts are not culturally neutral and that when authors write they consciously or subconsciously arrange the characters and plot to express a feeling. Tell students that when they are reading in a new language they need to be aware of the ways their own cultural group is being represented and how the majority culture is portrayed. Explain to students that authors can subtly express bias, romanticize, and cast aspersions on a specific cultural group and that by problematizing texts students can become aware of these opinions.
4. Demonstrate problematizing texts to students by using a book written in Spanish if you are teaching in the Spanish language and a book written in English if you are instructing students in English. An appropriate book for a demonstration is the English version *Click, Clack, Moo: Cows that Type* (Cronin, 2000) or the Spanish version *Clic, Clac, Muu: Vacas Escritoras* (Cronin, 2002).

5. Read the story to students. Divide the class into groups of three or four students with a proficient speaker of the language of instruction in each group. Have students retell the story in their own words to be certain that every student understands what has happened in the story.

6. Read the story a second time. After this reading, distribute to students copies of the English or Spanish version of the Problematizing Text Questions reproducibles on pages 111–112. Read the questions with the students, explaining what each one means in the context of the story. Since the concepts for problematizing are difficult for students to understand, provide an explanation in the language that students know best. An example of explanations both in English and Spanish follows.

♦ **How does the author represent social and cultural groups?**
Look at the groups that are represented in this story. We see the cows, the farmer, and the ducks. How does the author represent each group?

♦ **Is underlying bias present?**
Does the author show respect for each group? Are the animals given the same respect as the farmer? Does the author seem to portray one of the groups as smarter than the others?

♦ **Which groups represent power?**
Who has power in this story: the farmer, the cows, and/or the ducks? How is power changed in the story? How does the typewriter also represent power?

♦ **How are conflicts resolved and what does that say about humanity?**
The cows presented the conflict in the story by wanting their conditions to be improved. The farmer didn't want to make the changes until the cows withheld their milk. What does this say about people in power?

♦ **What has the author left unsaid?**
Are there parts of the story that the author didn't include in the story as it is written? What is left out? For example, do you think the farmer had a family? If he did, what role could they have had in the story? What else isn't part of the story?

♦ **What does this text reveal about our culture?**
Does this story say anything about the ways in which people behave in North America? Are there similarities to and differences from people in other countries with which you are familiar?

♦ **¿Cómo presenta el autor los varios grupos sociales y culturales en este texto?**
Fíjate en los grupos que están representatados en esta historia. Vemos vacas, el granjero, y los patos. ¿Cómo presenta el autor cada grupo?

♦ **¿Se observa parcialidad o prejuicios en el trasfondo de las palabras?**
¿Muestra el autor respeto por cada grupo? ¿Son los animales tratados con el mismo respeto que el granjero?
¿Parece el autor representar un grupo como más inteligente que los otros?

♦ **¿Cuáles grupos representan la imagen del poderío?**
¿Quién tiene poder en esta historia: el granjero, las vacas, y/o los patos?
¿Cómo cambia el poder en la historia?
¿Cómo la máquina de escribir representa poder?

♦ **¿Cómo se resuelven los conflictos y qué revelan estos procesos del ser humano?**
Las vacas presentaron el conflicto en la historia al querer mejorar su condición.
El granjero no quiso hacer los cambios hasta que las vacas negaron su leche.
¿Qué indica esto acerca de la gente en el poder?

◆ **¿Qué ha omitido o no mencionado el autor en este texto?**

¿Hay partes de la historia que el autor no incluyó en la historia escrita?

¿Qué se ha omitido?

Por ejemplo, ¿piensas que el granjero teniá una familia?

Si la tenía, ¿qué papel pudo su familia tener en la historia?

¿Qué más se ha omitido en la historia?

◆ **¿Qué aspectos de nuestra cultura se revelan en este texto?**

¿Dice esta historia algo acerca de la forma en que se comporta las personas en Norte América?

¿Existen parecidos o diferencias con personas de otros países con los que tienes familiaridad?

7. Have students select one of the questions to discuss in their groups. Circulate around the room so that you can provide ideas for groups that struggle with this strategy. Have students share ideas with the entire class that they discussed in their groups.

8. Repeat the Problematizing Text strategy frequently. As students become familiar with this strategy, encourage them to apply the Problematizing Text Questions to books and stories they read independently.

VARIATION

As you have students read texts critically, you can vary the questions so that students think about texts in different ways. Bean and Moni (2003) suggest that students ask questions such as the following when reading novels critically:

◆ Who is the ideal reader for this novel?

◆ Who gets to speak in this novel and who is silenced?

◆ What is left out of the novel?

◆ How else might the stories of the characters be told?

◆ How could this novel be rewritten to address cultural gaps?

NAME _____ DATE _____

PROBLEMATIZING TEXT QUESTIONS

1. How does the author represent social and cultural groups?

   _____
   _____
   _____

2. Is underlying bias present?

   _____
   _____
   _____

3. Which groups represent power?

   _____
   _____
   _____

4. How are conflicts resolved and what does that say about humanity?

   _____
   _____
   _____

5. What has the author left unsaid?

   _____
   _____
   _____

6. What does this text reveal about our culture?

   _____
   _____
   _____

NOMBRE _____ FECHA _____

PROBLEMATIZING TEXT QUESTIONS

1. ¿Cómo presenta el autor los varios grupos sociales y culturales en este texto?

_____

_____

_____

2. ¿Se observa parcialidad o prejuicios en el trasfondo de las palabras?

_____

_____

_____

3. ¿Cuáles grupos representan la imagen del poder?

_____

_____

_____

4. ¿Cómo se resuelven los conflictos y qué revelan acerca del ser humano?

_____

_____

_____

5. ¿Qué ha omitido o no mencionado el autor en este texto?

_____

_____

_____

6. ¿Qué aspectos de nuestra cultura son presentados en este texto?

_____

_____

_____

After Reading Strategies

eaders are not finished reading when they put down a text; they think about what they have read and even take action as a result of new knowledge. Students should also learn that they should extend their knowledge after reading by thinking about what they have read. Typically, however, when students read, they reach a provisional understanding of the text resulting in what has been called "good enough" reading (Mackey, 1997). Good-enough reading is reading that students do to complete an assignment without deep comprehension. Students who are learning a new language, either Spanish or English, fall prey to good-enough reading more often than do students reading their native language. According to Smith and Qi (2003, p. 54), "a student who reads fairly fluently may have only a vague idea of a text's contents." When students read stories in a new language, they may be able to read many of the words, get the gist of the passage, and feel successful about reading without having a thorough understanding of the text.

Cummins (2001) describes the reasons why students learning a new language have difficulty comprehending texts. He identifies three "faces" of language proficiency: conversational fluency, discrete language skills, and academic language. In short, conversational fluency is the ability to communicate in conversations using the second language. As anyone who has spoken a new language can attest, these conversations are often comprised of short phrases and punctuated with body language, hand gestures, and facial expressions—all used to get the meaning of the speaker across to the listener. Students typically can pick up conversational English or Spanish fairly quickly. Furthermore, students are able to learn the discrete language skills such as the alphabet and some of the rules that govern grammar fairly quickly. Academic language, however, is much more difficult. Cummins (2001) believes that new language learners often take from five to seven years to be able to communicate in the reading and writing that we expect in schools, including a rich comprehension of text.

The process of helping English-language learners achieve comprehension to the same degree as their native English-speaking peers can be hastened by having students recall texts and respond personally to texts and by helping students expand their vocabularies. Teachers can do this by modeling and demonstrating a variety of strategies that are included in this chapter. Taken along with strategies from other chapters in this book, these strategies can help students become better readers.

Activities after reading help students extend their understanding.

Estrellita: Accelerated Beginning Spanish Reading
www.estrellita.com

An educational reading program in Spanish for dominant Spanish speakers. It is a phonics based accelerated beginning Spanish reading program for primary bilingual classrooms.

Santillana USA
www.santillanusa.net

Sells English, bilingual, ESL/LED, and Spanish language materials.

SECTION 4.1 Recalling Text

Instructional Goal: **To help students recall important ideas and information from texts to support comprehension**

BACKGROUND

In order for students to construct meaning from texts, they need to recall enough of the texts to visualize and internalize the texts' ideas. Research indicates that identifying important information from texts can improve comprehension for all students (RAND Reading Study Group, 2002). When English-language learners have opportunities to recall texts, discuss what they've read, and process those thoughts, they are more likely to comprehend texts more deeply (Jiménez, 1997; Kottler & Kottler, 2002). However, some students learning a new language will need more scaffolding than other students do.

When students write a retelling, they deepen their understanding of the story.

Teachers frequently ask English-language learners to perform cognitive tasks, such as recalling texts, sequencing, and summarizing, without providing them with adequate demonstrations of the strategies. When English-language learners are asked to summarize texts, for example, they may have difficulty understanding what it means to "summarize." Therefore, English-language learners need to be taught these mental processes through demonstration and collaboration.

All students learning English need many opportunities to practice reading, writing, speaking, listening, and observing (Meeks & Austin, 2003). When instructing students who are learning a new language, teachers need to describe cognitive strategies in comprehensible language, repeatedly demonstrate these strategies, and provide students with collaborative experiences for them to use the targeted strategies in a nonthreatening situation. When English-language learners are provided with these types of instructional scenarios, they are more likely to comprehend the texts they are hearing and reading.

Barahona Center for the Study of Books in Spanish for Children and Adolescents
www.csusm.edu/csb/english
Provides lists of books in Spanish that can be used for classroom instruction.

4.1 Teaching Strategy 19

Sequencing

All texts have an organizational structure. In the case of narrative texts in both English and Spanish, texts follow a sequence of events. Texts that were originally written in Spanish might have a more complex story structure than those that were originally written in English, but they all have events that follow each other. Students should recall those events to improve their comprehension. When students recall texts, they have to identify the important parts of the story, and in doing so they begin to replay the events in the plot. This rehearsing of events helps students process information so they can better construct meaning after reading. Therefore, having students recall the sequence of events of a story is a strategy that can improve comprehension.

DIRECTIONS AND EXAMPLES

1. Tell students that when stories are written down the events will have the same order each time they read the book. Contrast written stories with stories students hear orally by discussing the differences between written and oral texts as in the example that follows.

> Many times our family members tell us stories. My grandfather tells our family stories all of the time. He often tells the same stories again and again about when he was young. Sometimes he even changes the order of the events in the story. That's because story telling is flexible. You can add to stories or change them each time you tell them.
>
> Stories you read in books are very different. They were written by authors who probably changed them a few times during the writing. Once they are printed, however, the stories will be the same each time they are read. To make a change in a printed story, the author would have to write it again and publish it in another version.

2. Explain to students that when they read they should pay close attention to the order of the events of the story because recalling the sequence of events can help them understand the story.

3. The term "sequence" may be new to many of the students. Explain to students the meaning of the term by saying something like the statements that follow.

> The word "sequence" means "to place in order." If I ask you the sequence of the morning activities, for example, you would list the pledge to the flag, the good morning song, the calendar, and so on. There is an order that we do these things every morning. If you are figuring out the sequence, then, you're finding the order of the events.

4. Duplicate and distribute one of the Sequencing reproducibles on pages 120–121. Use the English version if you are teaching the strategy in English or the Spanish version if you are teaching the strategy in Spanish.

5. Read students a short story either in English or in Spanish or demonstrate the strategy using the bilingual book *The Spirit of Tío Fernando: El espíritu de tío Fernando* (Levy, 1995). If you are instructing students in English,

read the English version or read the Spanish version if you are instructing students in Spanish.

6. Read a few pages at a time and have students identify the events in that section of the story. Write them on the board before students write them on their Sequencing sheets. Then continue reading more of the story and writing more of the events.

7. Examples using *The Spirit of Tío Fernando: El espíritu de tío Fernando* (Levy, 1995) follow.

The Spirit of Tío Fernando
1. Nando's mother woke him on the Day of the Dead so that he could honor tío Fernando.
2. Nando and his mother set up the altar.
3. Nando went to the market to purchase something to take to the cemetery.
4. Nando bought some candy and cookies.
5. The town had a fiesta.
6. Nando and his mother went to Fernando's tombstone.
7. Nando felt his uncle's spirit.

El espíritu de tío Fernando
1. La mamá de Nando lo despertó el Día de los Muertos para que pudiera honorar al tío Fernando.
2. Nando y su mamá montaron el altar.
3. Nando fue al mercado a comprar algo para llevar al cementerio.
4. Nando compró algunos caramelos y galletas.
5. El pueblo tuvo una fiesta.
6. Nando y su mama fueron a la tumba de Fernando.
7. Nando sintió el espíritu de su tío.

8. Demonstrate the sequencing strategy several times before you expect students to recall the sequence of events independently. Each time you model the strategy, remind students that they should try to recall the sequence of events when they read alone.

VARIATION

The Sequencing strategy can be used a number of ways. You can have students identify events in a story and have them write them in the correct order. Another way to use sequencing in a bilingual classroom is to have the most proficient readers identify the events and write them on the Sequencing reproducible and then cut the reproducible into strips. Students who are novice readers or who are struggling with the language can then read or listen to the story and arrange the cut apart sequence strips into the order of the story. A third way to use Sequencing strips is to use them as a prewriting activity before students write a story. Students can list events on the strips and then reorder them as they begin to draft their own stories.

NAME _____ DATE _____

SEQUENCING

_____

Title and Author

1.
2.
3.
4.
5.
6.
7.

NOMBRE _____ FECHA _____

SEQUENCING

_____

Título y Autor

1.
2.
3.
4.
5.
6.
7.

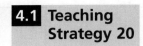

Magnet Summaries

Magnet Summaries (Buehl, 2001) is a scaffolded method of asking students to write a summary. Summary writing has been a popular strategy for recalling text for decades; however, the cognitive processes necessary for summary writing make this strategy questionable for students who are learning a new language. Magnet Summaries provide students with key terms that are necessary for recalling text, and when students are asked to write a summary, they tend to be more successful.

DIRECTIONS AND EXAMPLES

1. Tell students that you want them to recall texts by writing a magnet summary of a book or a passage they have read. Explain to students that writing a magnet summary is not the same thing as writing a book report but it is a way to remember something they have heard or read. To explain, you might make the following comments.

> Today we're going to work in small groups in order to recall a story I will read to you. When you recall a story, you can think about the events that occurred and restate the story in one or two sentences, which is called a summary. A summary does not include every detail in the story; it just states the main ideas. Most students need lots of practice before they can write summaries, so don't worry if you find this strategy difficult at first. After practice, you'll find writing summaries is easy!

2. Select a book or passage to read to students to demonstrate Magnet Summaries. Choose a book in English if you are instructing your students in English or choose a book in Spanish if you are instructing your students in Spanish or use the bilingual book *Brother Anansi and the Cattle Ranch: El hermano Anansi y el rancho de ganado* (Rohmer, 1989a) which is a folktale originating in Nicaragua.

3. Duplicate and distribute either the English or the Spanish version of the Magnet Summaries reproducibles on pages 124–125. Give each student a copy of the reproducible.

4. Read the book to students. Tell students that you want them to recall the story, from the beginning to the end. Explain to students that you will help them recall the story by providing them with key terms used in the story.

5. Write several words on the Magnet Words lines that represent key ideas in the story. Try to include words from the beginning, the middle, and the end of the story. If you need more words than fit in the blanks, draw additional blanks on the form.

6. Divide the class into groups of three or four students. Make sure a proficient speaker of the language of instruction is present in each group.

7. Read the Magnet Words with students. Have the students discuss the words in small groups so that they have a clear concept of the meaning of each word.

8. Discuss the words with students if necessary. For example, some students may not be familiar with the term "lottery," so you will need to describe lotteries and explain how the term is used in the story.
9. If students are successful discussing the words from the story, have them compose two or three sentences using the terms. Provide students with time to discuss possible sentences in groups before they write them on the form.
10. Ask students to volunteer Summary Sentences with the class. If students are not confident about their sentences, provide an example for them. Then have students write either their own sentences or your example on the line.

Magnet Words	Magnet Words
__lottery__ __cattle ranch__ __leaves__ __trick__	__lotería__ __hacienda de ganado__ __hojas__ __truco__
Summary Sentences	**Summary Sentences**
Brother Tiger won the lottery so Brother Anansi suggested they develop a cattle ranch. They bought cattle and pinned leaves on the cattle. Brother Anansi tricked Brother Tiger and got all the cattle.	*El hermano Tigre ganó la lotería, así que el hermano Anansi sugirió que crearan una hacienda de ganado. Ellos comprarón el ganado y colocarón hojas en el ganado. El hermano Anansi engaño al hermano Tigre y obturo todo el ganado.*

11. Have students read the Summary Sentences and decide whether the sentences accurately retell the story. Revise the Summary Sentences if necessary.
12. Use Magnet Summaries in the whole class and in small groups several times before expecting students to complete summaries independently. Remind students that when they read they should identify key terms in their minds and retell the story in order to remember it.

ASSESSMENT IDEA

To determine whether or not students comprehended a story, Hurley and Tinajero (2001) suggest you have students retell the story to you without the Magnet Summary words. If students are able to retell the main parts of the story without difficulty, have them write their retellings. If they have difficulty writing in English, have students tell you the story orally. Retelling reinforces oral communication as well as gives you information about how well students have comprehended the story. If students are not able to retell the story, have them reread the story and try again.

NAME _____ DATE _____

MAGNET SUMMARIES

Magnet Words

_____   _____

_____   _____

_____   _____

Summary Sentences

_____

_____

_____

_____

_____

Magnet Words

_____   _____

_____   _____

_____   _____

Summary Sentences

_____

_____

_____

_____

_____

Magnet Words

_____   _____

_____   _____

_____   _____

Summary Sentences

_____

_____

_____

_____

_____

Magnet Words

_____   _____

_____   _____

_____   _____

Summary Sentences

_____

_____

_____

_____

_____

NOMBRE _____ FECHA _____

MAGNET SUMMARIES

Palabras Imánes	**Palabras Imánes**
_____ _____	_____ _____
_____ _____	_____ _____
_____ _____	_____ _____
Oraciones Resumen	**Oraciones Resumen**
_____	_____
_____	_____
_____	_____
_____	_____
_____	_____

Palabras Imánes	**Palabras Imánes**
_____ _____	_____ _____
_____ _____	_____ _____
_____ _____	_____ _____
Oraciones Resumen	**Oraciones Resumen**
_____	_____
_____	_____
_____	_____
_____	_____
_____	_____
_____	_____

4.1 Teaching Strategy 21

Plus, Minus, Interesting (PMI)

When students recall text, they also make value judgments about their reading. You can encourage this type of analysis by teaching students the strategy Plus, Minus, Interesting (PMI) (deBono, 1976). After reading, students recall ideas from the text and respond to the ideas by listing them on a chart. The combined process of recall and assigning value judgments helps students comprehend texts.

DIRECTIONS AND EXAMPLES

1. Tell students that they should think about what they read by recalling parts of the story. Explain to students that there are a number of ways to recall texts—some include sequencing, summarizing, and other strategies students have learned. Tell students that sometimes they can recall parts of texts by deciding which parts were positive, which were negative, and which were interesting.

2. Duplicate and distribute one of the PMI charts on pages 129–130. Choose the Spanish version if you are instructing students in Spanish or the English version if your language of instruction is English. Make sure that your instructions are clear and comprehensible. Don't hesitate to repeat directions several times until your meaning is clear.

3. Select a text to read to students or to have them read alone. You can use any type of text for this activity: fictional, informational, poems, or plays, or you can use the bilingual book of poems *A Movie in My Pillow: Una película en mi almohada* (Argueta, 2001). Jorge Argueta is a poet and teacher who was born in El Salvador. Elizabeth Gómez, who was born in Mexico City, drew the illustrations for this book. Read the poems in the language that you are using for instruction in your class.

4. Have students write the title of the book in the top section of the PMI reproducible. Then tell students that you will be asking them to think about a text by recalling and responding to different parts of the text.

5. Read the text to students or have them read it independently. If students are reading the book themselves, make sure they are reading in the language of instruction. (After the lesson, you can have students reread the poems in their native language if desired.)

6. Ask students what in the book they found was positive, what they found was negative, and what they found was interesting. Reassure students that there are no "right answers" for this activity but that different students will have different ideas.

7. Demonstrate how to recall the positive ideas from texts. Explain to students that events in the story can be positive or negative and that they need to recall some of these events. Remind students that each one of them might find different ideas to put in the positive column. Provide an example by saying something like the words that follow.

> After reading the book *A Movie in My Pillow: Una película en mi almohada,* I thought several things were really positive, so I'll start with that. In many of the poems, I was struck

by how much Jorge loved his family. I'll put that in the box under positive.

Another thing I noticed was that the poet found beauty in so many things. When he didn't have enough to eat in El Salvador, he looked at the stars and "the stars were our soup." I'll write that down too because I think it shows how Jorge found beauty everywhere.

8. Demonstrate how to recall the negative ideas from texts. Tell students that stories they read will often have ideas or events that are negative. Remind students that their idea of a negative event might be different from others in the class. Provide an example, such as the following one.

I remember several negative things from the book. Jorge had to leave his family because of the war. I'll write that down first. I'll also write down that he had to leave his best friend Neto. I think that was definitely negative.

9. Tell students that sometimes ideas or events are neither positive nor negative but can be classified as interesting. Remind students that what is interesting to them might not be interesting to someone else. Encourage students to recall the parts of the text that they think are interesting as in the example that follows.

As I read *A Movie in My Pillow: Una película en mi almohada*, I thought several things were interesting that I want to write down. I thought it was really interesting that Jorge's grandmother could speak Nahautl, so I'll write that down. I also thought it was interesting that there are so many languages spoken in San Francisco.

10. Show students the PMI chart with your entries in it and then tell students that their charts will have different ideas written in them.

Title: *A Movie in My Pillow*		
Plus +	Minus −	Interesting
Jorge loved his family and missed them when he came to San Francisco. Jorge found beauty in many things.	Jorge left El Salvador with his father. He had to leave the rest of his family behind. Jorge had to leave his best friend Neto.	Jorge's grandmother speaks Nahautl. In San Francisco people speak English and Spanish and they also speak other languages such as Chinese and Arabic.

Título: *Una película en mi almohada*		
Mas +	**Menos −**	**Interesante**
Jorge quería a su familia y la extrañabá cuando vino a San Francisco. Jorge encontró muchas cosas bonitas.	Jorge se marchó de El Salvador con su padre. Tuvo que dejar al resto de su familia allá. Jorge tuvo que dejar a su mejor amigo Neto.	La abuelita de Jorge habla Nahautl. En San Francisco la gente habla inglés y español y también otras lenguas como chino y árabe.

11. Have students complete their own charts in small groups or independently. You may have to give students a great deal of support before they are ready to use the PMI charts on their own. Provide examples and demonstrations of the PMI until students are able to use this strategy when they read independently. Remind students that when they use the PMI strategy they are recalling ideas and events from their reading and making a value judgment about them. Also remind students that using strategies such as the PMI will help them comprehend their reading.

VARIATION

The Plus, Minus, Interesting chart can be used in a number of ways. Some student might find all three columns overwhelming, so you can have students read to find one of the areas on the chart. For example, you might have students just look for things that they thought were positive, or you might have students record just the ideas they found interesting.

NAME _____ DATE _____

PLUS, MINUS, INTERESTING (PMI)

Title:		
Plus +	Minus –	Interesting

NOMBRE _____ FECHA _____

PLUS, MINUS, INTERESTING (PMI)

Título:		
Más +	Menos –	Interesante

SECTION 4.2	# Responding Personally

Instructional Goal: **To provide students with the opportunity to respond to their reading through a variety of media**

BACKGROUND

Students can deepen their comprehension of text by participating in activities that elicit their personal responses. According to Echevarria and Graves (2003), students who are learning a new language are more successful and have a bet-

ter attitude toward schooling when they are allowed to use the background that they have to construct their own meanings of texts. When students respond to texts, they are bringing their background knowledge and experience to the learning situation (see Rosenblatt, 1978). Responding personally does not entail a complete understanding of the story; instead it allows students to combine their knowledge of the text with their own background to construct meaning that is richer than was previously held.

Teachers often have students respond to text through writing in journals, but Altwerger and Ivener (1994) caution teachers of students learning a new language that ELL students often have feelings of inadequacy when they are asked to partici-

Students can respond to their reading through drawing.

pate in classroom activities, such as writing, that require a knowledge of academic English. Students who are leaning a new language are typically more successful when they can participate in types of learning activities other than writing, such as dramatic presentations, art, and music. Using literacies other than reading and writing can indeed further students' comprehension of text and proficiency in language. Therefore, students who are learning a new language can benefit from responding personally to text through various strategies using a range of modalities.

Multicultural Pavilion
http://curry.edschool.Virginia.edu/go/multicultural/
Geared to the needs of educators, this website offers a tremendous amount of material about multicultural identity in the classroom. Research articles, classroom resources, a discussion forum, and a listserv are just a few of the kinds of resources to be found here.

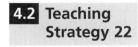

4.2 Teaching Strategy 22

Sketch to Stretch

Sketch to Stretch (Short, Harste, & Burke, 1996) is a strategy that evokes artistic personal responses from students about their readings. This strategy applies to all types of texts: fiction, informational, poetry, rhymes, and songs. It also helps students visualize their texts and create meaning as they read. When using Sketch to Stretch, students are asked to draw a sketch after reading or listening to a text, showing what the passage means to them and/or how the passage makes them feel. English and Spanish language learners find Sketch to Stretch very valuable. Often students learning a new language comprehend what they hear or read but have difficulty describing their understanding in the language of instruction. Sketch to Stretch allows students to express their thoughts in pictures rather than words.

DIRECTIONS AND EXAMPLES

1. Select a text for students to hear or read in your language of instruction. If your students are learning to read in English, read an English text; if your students are learning to read in Spanish, chose a Spanish text. If you have a classroom context where some students are learning English and others are learning Spanish, read from a bilingual book such as *Diez deditos: Ten Little Fingers* (Orozco, 1997). That way you can use the same text and strategy for both groups.

2. Read part of the text to students and model how you are responding to the text as you read. For example, if you were reading the poem "Sí Se Puede! Yes, I Can!" for your students, you would say something like the words that follow.

> I was reading this poem about how I am unique, special, intelligent, and loving. That started me thinking about ways in which I'm unique and special. I think maybe I'm unique because I am the only girl in my family and the only one who likes to draw. I have a husband and three sons. I also have four brothers, so I'm very special in my family. I'm also loving, especially to my grandparents, parents, husband, and children. I also love my dogs. I can sit for hours with my children on my lap and my dogs at my feet. I sing to them, stroke their hair, tickle them, and enjoy being with them. I can say that I really do believe that I'm special when I think about my family.
>
> When I read this poem, I think about myself and my family, and I picture myself with them. I'm visualizing these things as I read. When I picture things in my mind, I have a better understanding of my reading.

3. After describing to students what you thought as you read the text, introduce the strategy Sketch to Stretch. Explain to students that you can draw a picture of your feelings and that these pictures represent your personal response as your read. Explain this idea by remarking as follows.

> I'm going to sketch what I was thinking as I read this poem. First I'm going to draw myself sitting on my couch with a book. Then I'll add my three boys sitting with me. The baby will be on my lap, and I'll have my other two sons on either side of

me. We'll all be smiling and laughing. I'll have my dog at my feet. The dog will be wagging its tail.

This picture will allow me to remember what I was thinking and the connections I made when I read this poem. If I read the poem again, I might think of something else. I'll just sketch these pictures in my journal to remind me of my thoughts. I'm not going to color the pictures or hang them up in the room. Instead, I'll share them with a few of my friends.

4. Read the second stanza of the poem. This one is about achieving goals. Draw a picture on the board or on an overhead transparency of your thinking as you read the poem. An example follows.

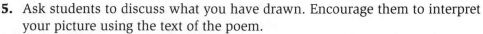

5. Ask students to discuss what you have drawn. Encourage them to interpret your picture using the text of the poem.

6. Duplicate and distribute one of the Sketch to Stretch reproducibles on pages 135–136. Use either the English version or the Spanish version. Read the entire poem again and have students draw their thoughts and feelings in the box as they read. Remind students that they don't have to be artists to draw in their journals but that their drawings should represent their thoughts as they listen to the poem. Give students several minutes to complete their drawings.

7. When students have finished their sketches, divide the class into small groups. Have students share their sketches with their classmates. Have the students looking at a sketch respond to it by completing the following statements.

> I think this sketch is about . . .
>
> I think the artist feels . . .
>
> I think the artist has made a connection to . . .

8. After students have finished their discussions, have them write about their sketches by completing the following statements.

> This sketch is about . . .
>
> I feel . . .
>
> I made a connection to . . .

9. Encourage students to share their final thoughts with their groups' members.

ASSESSMENT IDEA

You can tell whether students understood their reading by the sketches that they drew. If the sketches do not have anything to do with the story, remind students that they need to make a link between their drawings and the story they heard or read. Then give students a second chance to sketch something that relates to the story. If students' second attempt still does not relate to the story, have students reread the story concentrating on understanding the printed word.

NAME _____ DATE _____

SKETCH TO STRETCH

This sketch is about _____

_____

_____

I feel _____

_____

_____

I made a connection to _____

_____

_____

NOMBRE _____ FECHA _____

SKETCH TO STRETCH

```
┌─────────────────────────────────────────────┐
│                                               │
│                                               │
│                                               │
│                                               │
│                                               │
│                                               │
└─────────────────────────────────────────────┘
```

Este es un dibujo acerca de _____

_____

_____

Siento _____

_____

_____

Me conecta con _____

_____

_____

4.2 Teaching
Strategy 23

Two-Column Response Chart

Many teachers have students respond to their reading through writing, and this strategy is a good one for all students. Some students who are learning a new language, however, can have difficulty with open-ended assignments such as journal writing. Another method to use with students whom you want to respond to their reading through writing is a Two-Column Response Chart (Ollmann, 1991/1992). A Two-Column Response Chart has students identify a passage or a situation from the text that has meaning for them. As students identify meaningful passages, they begin connecting their background knowledge to the text, which improves the possibility of deepened comprehension. Then students write responses to those passages or situations. When students personally respond to passages or situations that they have identified as meaningful, they are more likely to be able to write about their feelings and experiences, resulting in reaching deeper levels of comprehension of the text.

DIRECTIONS AND EXAMPLE

1. Identify a story to read to students or to have students read independently. If your students are learning English, read the story in English. If your students are learning Spanish, read the story in Spanish. If you are reading a bilingual book to students, make every effort to keep your reading and instruction in the language you are trying to teach. An example of a bilingual book that is appropriate for this strategy is *Friends from the Other Side: Amigos del otro lado* written by the Mexican-American author Gloria Anzaldua (1993) and illustrated by Consuelo Mendez, a painter and graphic artist from Venezuela.

2. Duplicate and distribute one of the copies of the Two-Column Response Charts on pages 139–140. Use the English reproducible if you are conducting the class in English and a Spanish reproducible if you are conducting the class in Spanish.

3. Tell students that this chart will be a place for them to write personal responses. Explain to students that when they read a book or listen to a story they should identify passages, ideas, and situations that are interesting. Point out the left column where students can write down ideas from the story. Then point out the right column. Tell students that the right column is for them to write a personal response to the story. Emphasize to students that when they are writing a response they should write what they think and feel about the identified passage.

4. Read the story *Friends from the Other Side: Amigos del otro lado* to students and fill out the Two-Column Response Chart with them as in the example that follows.

Ideas from Story	Personal Response
Prietita asked Joaquin whether he came "from the other side" because she noticed that his Spanish was not the same as hers.	*I remember when my aunt and uncle from Mexico came to live with us. They seemed very different from our family even though my uncle is my dad's brother. Their Spanish was not a lot different from ours but a little. I think we speak a lot of English with our Spanish.*
Joaquin was scared when the Border Patrol (La Migra) began searching the houses. He found his mother and ran to hide.	*I've never seen La Migra but I've heard lots of stories. When my grandfather came to this country, he had to cross the border alone. He had to keep hidden so that he wouldn't get caught. He was so very afraid of La Migra, and he still is afraid of them even though he now is a United States citizen.*
The herb woman said that Prietita was ready to learn how to use her herbs after she helped hide Joaquin and his mother.	*My mother knows lots about herbs and healing too. She's teaching me all of the time. One day a wasp stung me, and mom put something really soothing on my skin. She showed me how to make the medicine so that I can use it by myself someday.*

5. Read the story a second time and have students identify their own passages and ideas from the story. Have students write these ideas in the left-hand column. Then have students write their responses in the right-hand column. Encourage students to write about their thoughts, feelings, emotions, and personal experiences.

6. Have students respond to their reading using the Two-Column Response Chart regularly. You might have to use the strategy several times in a group before students feel comfortable using it on their own. Strive to make this strategy one that students use when they read independently.

NAME _____ DATE _____

TWO-COLUMN RESPONSE CHART

Ideas from Story	Personal Responses

NOMBRE _____ FECHA _____

TWO-COLUMN RESPONSE CHART

Ideas de la Historia	Respuestas Personales

4.2 Teaching Strategy 24

Drama Frame

"Process drama is a method of teaching and learning that involves students in imaginary, unscripted, and spontaneous scenes" (Schneider & Jackson, 2000, p. 38). Process drama can be used in a number of ways: it can be used before, during, and after reading. When used as a prereading activity, process drama can help students imagine stories and plots that they can use in their writing. During reading students can use process drama to help them interpret what they have read so far. Probably the most useful way to use process drama with students learning a new language, however, is as a response to reading. Students who are able to understand some aspect of their reading can deepen their understanding by thinking about how to "act it out." When students act out a story, they need to think about the story, converse with their peers, and interpret what they have read. Drama, therefore, is a strategy that is valuable for all students but is especially appropriate for students who are learning a new language.

When students are preparing for dramatic interpretations, Lenski and Johns (2004) suggest that they use a Drama Frame. Drama Frames are an organizational tool that students can use to record ideas for process drama. The Drama Frames used most frequently have sections for characters, setting, plot, and dialogue, but they can be adapted for other components of drama.

DIRECTIONS AND EXAMPLES

1. Tell students that you value their interpretations of their readings and that you will be giving them the opportunity to "act out" a story they have read by using process drama.

2. Explain to students that they will not need a script while participating in process drama. Remind students that actors on television and in movies usually have to memorize a script before they begin acting. Tell students that for process drama they will be given roles, scenes, and action but that they will have to invent the dialogue as they go.

3. Select a theme, unit of study, or a book students have read as the centerpiece for the drama. Provide instructions for students about how to orchestrate process drama as in the example that follows using the bilingual book *Angel's Kite: La estrella de angel* (Blanco, 1994). When using this example, use the English text if your students are learning English or the Spanish text if they are learning Spanish. Because process drama involves dramatic representation of a story and the creation of dialogue, it is particularly suited for instruction in the language that students are learning.

> I'm going to read the book *Angel's Kite* to you today. This story was written by Alberto Blanco, one of Mexico's most outstanding poets. The illustrations are by Rodolfo Morales who is one of Mexico's greatest living artists. I'm going to read to you in English today. While I read, I'd like you to think about the characters and the plot. After I read the story, I'm going to ask you to "act it out."

4. Duplicate and distribute one of the Drama Frame reproducibles on pages 144–145. Use the English example if you are teaching the lesson in English and the Spanish example if you are teaching the lesson in Spanish.

5. Point out the components of the Drama Frame and explain each section as follows.

> You'll notice that the Drama Frame is divided into four sections. The first one is labeled *characters.* You know that the term *characters* is the word we use for the people or animals that are in the story. As I read, I'd like you to think about the characters in the story and jot down any notes or ideas that you have. For example, you might be thinking about what the characters should wear or how the characters should act.
>
> The term in the second column is *setting.* The setting is the time and place of the story. As I read, you can write down the setting of this story, but you can also write down other ideas you have about the setting. For example, you might write down ideas for props or scenery.
>
> The third term is the *plot.* The plot is the action of the story. Books in English typically present some sort of problem that the characters need to solve. Write down what you remember of the plot as I read.
>
> Finally, think about *dialogue.* The dialogue is the words that characters say to each other. You'll be making up some dialogue when you act out the story, but you might write down some ideas as you listen.

6. Read the story to students once so that they hear the plot and a second time for them to write notes on the Drama Frame. Ask students if they want any parts of the story repeated for a third time. An example of an entry on a Drama Frame for *Angel's Kite: La estrella de angel* follows.

Characters	Setting	Plot	Dialogue
Angel	Small town Mexico Present time	Church bell was gone. Angel made kites. Angel made a kite with symbols from the town including the church bell. Town kite flew away. Angel waited for the kite to descend. The kite lost its symbols but Angel heard a bell ringing. Church bell reappeared.	Angel talking to himself as he made the kites Angel telling everyone about the symbols on the town kite Angel yelling and crying when the kite flew away Angel exclaiming when he found the kite

Characters	Setting	Plot	Dialogue
			Angel saying how happy and thankful he is for the church bell to be returned
Angel's dogs: Lobo, Chino, Rabito		Stayed with Angel through everything	Angel calls dogs to come with him as he ran toward the kite
Children in town		Played with kites Followed Angel	Tell Angel how beautiful the kites are Talk about the town kite
Angel's friends		Went with Angel to try to find the kite Did not wait until the kite came down Celebrated the return of the bell	Tell Angel to leave the kite alone Ask Angel to come home with them and play soccer

7. Divide the class into groups of four or five students. Make sure a proficient speaker of the language of instruction is present in each group. Tell students to develop short dramatic presentations, or skits, of a part of the story. Reinforce the idea that the groups do not need to act out the entire story.

8. Once students have an idea about what they want to dramatize, tell them that they will be making up much of the dialogue as they act. Explain to students that actors typically say lines that are already written but that you want them to make up the dialogue themselves.

9. Give students time to practice their skits several times. Remind students that as they practice their skits they will be thinking more deeply about the story they heard and they will be practicing dialogue in a new language.

10. Encourage students to identify additional books to use with the Drama Frame. Once students have become comfortable with process drama, have them read different books in small groups and present their skits to the class. Using drama in this way can also introduce students to new books to read.

VARIATIONS

Students can also use the Drama Frame as a prewriting organizer for fictional texts. When students use the Drama Frame, they think about the different components of a story, which helps them in the planning stages of writing. Students can also act out the story before writing to give them a sense of the story and the dialogue they could write. If students plan and act out stories before beginning to write, they are able to use their mental resources to compose sentences and apply their grammatical knowledge during the process of writing. Second-language learners especially need to structure their stories before they begin to write so that they are able to fluently express their thoughts.

NAME _____ DATE _____

DRAMA FRAME

Characters	Setting	Plot	Dialogue

NOMBRE _____ FECHA _____

DRAMA FRAME

Personajes	Escenario	Trama	Diálogo

Reinforcing and Expanding Vocabulary

> *Instructional Goal:* **To reinforce vocabulary words students have learned through reading**

BACKGROUND

The purpose of vocabulary instruction is for students to use their word knowledge to communicate and comprehend. Often, students have a limited view of what it means to know and learn a word. This is typically promoted by teaching instruction that may fail to help students realize that they may know more about words than they realize and that acquiring a word goes beyond being able to provide a fixed definition for a given term. Students fail to realize that the lexical nature of language requires that readers understand the meanings of words in relation to other words and in relation to the situations or contexts in which the words are used.

This situation becomes clearly evident when working with English-language learners (ELLs). Frequently, instruction given to ELLs focuses on language structures and does not help students use vocabulary knowledge to become proficient comprehenders of text (Valdéz, 1998). In a study of multilingual students, Kong and Pearson (2003) found that students who were engaged in vocabulary development through an authentic reading, writing, and conversing activity were able to learn the meanings of words more effectively. One approach to reinforcing and expanding vocabulary in ELLs, as well as for English-speaking students, is for students to actively use new vocabulary words in meaningful ways.

Students have individual thresholds for the numbers of times they need to use a word before it becomes part of their lexicons. Some students will learn vocabulary through reading and writing while others will need more examples and direct instruction. This holds true for both native English speakers and English-language learners. Gersten and Jiménez (1994), for example, found that ELLs retain new vocabulary words when they are taught in depth. Therefore, teachers should provide ELLs with the necessary time and assistance so that they learn the meanings of new words (Echevarria & Graves, 2003). The time that a Spanish-speaking student takes to learn new words in English may be more or less than English-speaking students. Conversely, students who are learning Spanish vocabulary terms also take different amounts of time to learn words. Learning new words depends on the context and the student.

Teachers often ask which words to select for vocabulary instruction. Beck, McKeown, and Kucan (2002) developed a system that classifies vocabulary words into three tiers. The first tier contains basic words: words that are so familiar that they do not need instruction. Words such as "family," "house," and "car" are Tier One words. Teachers do not need to teach Tier One words to students as vocabulary words. These words may need to be taught to students learning a second language, but they can be taught using simple translation

These students are proud of the new words they have learned.

activities. Tier Two words contain words that are of high frequency in reading, writing, speaking, and listening and that can be found in several subject areas. These words also need explanation and teaching because students may not learn the meanings of these words by reading them in context. Examples of Tier Two words are "precious," "ordinary," and "wonder." Tier Three consists of words that are used infrequently and that students need to know for a specific content area such as the words "isthmus," "neutron," and "skipper." These words might be taught so that students can understand a specific lesson, but Beck, McKeown, and Kucan (2002) contend that Tier Two words should be the types of vocabulary words that make up the bulk of vocabulary instruction. They suggest that Tier Two words have high usability so that students who learn Tier Two words will have a communicative advantage.

Selecting words for vocabulary instruction that have high usability makes sense for both English and Spanish learners. When teachers spend their instructional time helping students learn, reinforce, and expand their vocabularies, they should select words that students will encounter in multiple texts. Instruction for vocabulary words, however, should not merely consist of having students superficially write words in sentences or copy out definitions. Vocabulary instruction that fosters long-term use needs to engage students in thinking of words in multiple texts, contexts, and modalities.

Bilingual Language and Literacy
www.home.sprintmail.com/~peggyriehl/prbilang.htm
Gives links to sites on bilingual literacy.

4.3 Teaching Strategy 25

Vocabulary People Search

One of the most effective methods of reinforcing vocabulary words is through the use of these words in authentic conversations. Students who are learning English often need additional experiences in pronouncing words and using them in context (Haver, 2003). Activities such as the Vocabulary People Search can provide students with ways to talk about words with their peers in academic situations. The Vocabulary People Search is an adaptation of Hemmrich, Lim, and Neel's (1994) People Search. In a Vocabulary People Search, students use a list of vocabulary words that have been previously introduced to find other students who have knowledge about these words. This activity gives students an opportunity to walk around the classroom and converse with each other about the words they are learning. The Vocabulary People Search is a valuable strategy for every type of classroom, including English- or Spanish-only classrooms, bilingual classrooms, and dual language classrooms.

DIRECTIONS AND EXAMPLES

1. Identify five vocabulary words that students have learned that need reinforcement. The words could be either in Spanish or in English. Remember that you will be asking students to discuss the words' definitions rather than merely having students give you a translation. List the words on a sheet of paper. An example of a Spanish list from *Gathering the Sun: An Alphabet in Spanish and English* by Alma Flor Ada (1997) that you might use if your students are learning vocabulary in Spanish follows. (*Gathering the Sun*, a book written in both Spanish and English, is used for the example. When you use the strategy, you should use books written in the language you are using for instruction, either Spanish or English.)

Spanish Words	English Words
Compañeros	Companions
Transplanta	Transplant
Luminosas	Shining
Sueño	Dream
Unidos	United

2. Show the list of words to students. Ask students how many of them could give a definition of one of these words. Be sure to paraphrase your question. You may first use more complex language (questions containing embedded questions), but then be sure to use simplified language to meet the needs of students of varying degrees of proficiency. Remind students that a definition explains the meaning of the word by saying something like the sentences that follow.

> How many of you know what the word "compañeros" means? You know that "compañeros" could have many meanings and that meanings differ according to how the word is used. You might have heard your grandfather use "compañeros" to mean a fellow worker in the coffee plantations, or you might have heard your mother use the word when she talked about her friends at the community center. Talk with your friends right now about your background with the word "compañeros."

3. After students have discussed their knowledge of the word "compañeros," read the first sentence in the book *Gathering the Sun: An Alphabet in Spanish and English* to remind students how Alma Flor Ada used "compañeros" in her book. Again, be sure to read the story in the language in which you are conducting the lesson. Then have students talk about the meaning of the word as it was used in the story.

4. Have students develop a brief definition of the word "compañeros" as it was used in the story. You may have students skim through the text and identify all of the instances where the word was used. Then you may ask

students to give you a definition of the word. An example of a definition for "compañeros" could be "a person with whom one works."

5. Explain to students that they have just given a definition of the word "compañeros" that fits the story that they read.

6. Tell students that they will be engaging in an activity called Vocabulary People Search that helps them discuss and define words that they have already learned. Duplicate and distribute one of the reproducibles on pages 150–151. Use the Spanish version if you are teaching vocabulary in Spanish or use the English version if you are teaching vocabulary in English.

7. Once students have a copy of the Vocabulary People Search, give directions using the statements that follow.

> I'm going to give each of you a list of words that we have previously discussed and that you've read in the book *Gathering the Sun: An Alphabet in Spanish and English.* I want you to walk around the room and ask your classmates to help you write a definition for the word. You and a classmate together should discuss the word and write a short definition that you think best defines the word as it was used in the story. You can look back at the book if you want to see how it was used. Have your classmate record his or her signature in the space next to the word and then write the definition in the line provided.

8. Give students ample time to complete the activity. As students work, circulate around the room, reminding them to use either Spanish or English, whichever language you are using for the activity. Remind students that they are expanding their use of language when they engage in discussions.

VARIATION

The Vocabulary People Search can be adapted for learning translations of words for students who are learning either English or Spanish. When using the strategy for translation, arrange words in the primary language on the left-hand side of the page. Have students gather signatures of their classmates who can translate the words into the secondary language. Include a blank for the translated word as in the example below.

Vocabulary Word	Classmate's Signature	Translated Word
Naranjas	*Marta L.*	Oranges
Despierta	*Juan*	Wake up

NAME _____ DATE _____

VOCABULARY PEOPLE SEARCH

1. _____   _____
           Vocabulary Word   Name of Classmate

   Definition _____

   _____

2. _____   _____
           Vocabulary Word   Name of Classmate

   Definition _____

   _____

3. _____   _____
           Vocabulary Word   Name of Classmate

   Definition _____

   _____

4. _____   _____
           Vocabulary Word   Name of Classmate

   Definition _____

   _____

5. _____   _____
           Vocabulary Word   Name of Classmate

   Definition _____

   _____

6. _____   _____
           Vocabulary Word   Name of Classmate

   Definition _____

   _____

NOMBRE _____ FECHA _____

VOCABULARY PEOPLE SEARCH

1. _____   _____
                          Palabra   Nombre del Compañero/a

Definición _____

_____

2. _____   _____
                          Palabra   Nombre del Compañero/a

Definición _____

_____

3. _____   _____
                          Palabra   Nombre del Compañero/a

Definición _____

_____

4. _____   _____
                          Palabra   Nombre del Compañero/a

Definición _____

_____

5. _____   _____
                          Palabra   Nombre del Compañero/a

Definición _____

_____

6. _____   _____
                          Palabra   Nombre del Compañero/a

Definición _____

_____

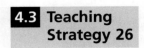

Teaching Strategy 26

Concept Circles

Most students will need many experiences with words before new vocabulary terms are part of their lexicons. Strategies such as Concept Circles (Vacca & Vacca, 2003) can provide students with opportunities to think about new words and how these words are related to other words they know. Concept Circles are simply circles divided into three sections that can be used in a variety of ways to expand vocabulary knowledge (Johns, Lenski, & Berglund, 2003). One of the ways to use Concept Circles is to have students think of three words or terms that are related to a concept that is taught during vocabulary lessons. Students who attend classes either in Spanish or English can benefit from this strategy.

DIRECTIONS AND EXAMPLES

1. Identify several vocabulary words that represent a concept that you want students to learn. For example, a concept vocabulary word from *The Woman Who Outshone the Sun: The Legend of Lucia Zenteno* (Zubizaarreta, Rohmer, & Schecter, 1991) is the word "respect," or in Spanish "respeto."
2. If you are teaching the class in English, write the word "respect" on the chalkboard. If you are teaching the class in Spanish, write the word "respeto."
3. Under the word, draw a circle divided into three sections similar to the one that follows.
4. Ask students to think of words or phrases that are related to the term "respect" or "respeto." For example, you might instruct students using the following statements.

> You learned about "respect" when we read *The Woman Who Outshone the Sun: The Legend of Lucia Zenteno.* In this story, we learned about Lucia Zenteno, whom the village people did not treat with respect. What are some words that describe the term "respect." Elicit a variety of answers and write them in the concept circle as follows.

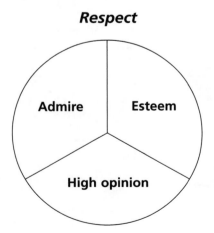

Respect

5. Explain to students that the words in the Concept Circle all relate to the main concept "respect." Tell students that Concept Circles can help them think of words they know that are related.

6. Write a second Concept Circle on the board, this time writing two of the words in the circle and leaving the main concept blank. For example, if you used the word "drought" ("sequía" in Spanish) from *The Woman Who Outshone the Sun: The Legend of Lucia Zenteno,* you might use the terms "dry," "no rain," or "lack of water." Fill in two of the spaces in the Concept Circle with related terms as follows.

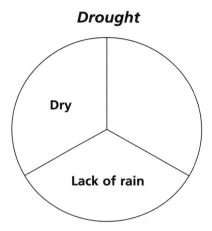

Drought

Dry

Lack of rain

7. Ask students to fill in the third section of the Concept Circle and to think of a vocabulary word from the story that describes the three terms written in the Concept Circle. The concept is "drought."

8. Use the reproducibles on pages 154–155 to help students develop their knowledge of concepts and related terms and thus reinforce and expand their vocabulary in the targeted language.

NAME _____ DATE _____

CONCEPT CIRCLES

Directions

1. Read the terms listed in the Concept Circles below.
2. Write in additional words that fit the concept in the circle.
3. Write the name of the concept in the line above the circle.

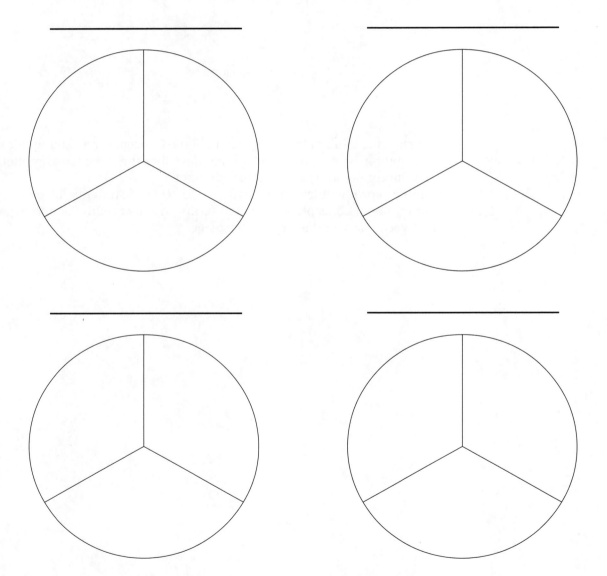

NOMBRE _____ FECHA _____

CONCEPT CIRCLES

Instrucciones

1. Lee los términos que aparecen en los Concept Circles abajo.
2. Escribe palabras adicionales relacionadas con el concepto adentro del círculo.
3. Escribe el nombre del concepto en la línea sobre el círculo.

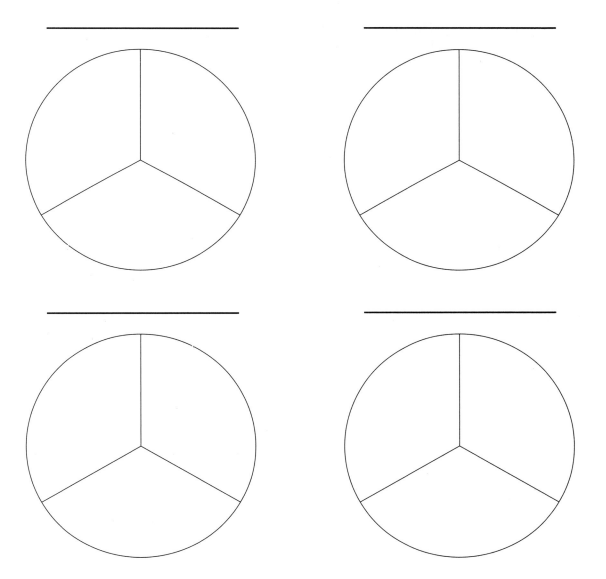

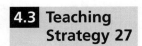

Word Storm

In order to reinforce and expand a student's vocabulary, teachers need to help students think of ways that they can adapt new words to other situations. Teachers often assign students to write vocabulary words in sentences, and although this is a good idea, students typically need more experience with words before being able to accomplish this goal. Students who are learning a second language especially need additional practice with a word's meanings before they are able to use the word in writing. A strategy that provides additional experiences with words is Word Storm (Klemp, 1994). Word Storm is a structured method of guiding students to think of words in different ways so they can ultimately use them in writing.

DIRECTIONS AND EXAMPLES

1. Identify two or three words from the list of vocabulary words students are learning that you believe will be valuable for students to use when they write.
2. Tell students that they will be focusing on just a few words from your vocabulary list and explain that you expect students to use the words you have selected in their writing.
3. Duplicate and distribute one of the Word Storm reproducibles on pages 158–159. Use the English version if you are teaching the lesson in English or use the Spanish version if your students are learning new vocabulary in Spanish.

4. Provide an example of the strategy Word Storm using the book *In My Family: En mi familia* by Carmen Lomas Garza (1996). This book is written in both Spanish and English so it can be used as a sample for lessons in either language. When you teach the strategy, however, you will probably want to use a book printed in either Spanish or English.
5. Make a transparency of the Word Storm reproducible that you are using. On the first line write the word "ignited." Tell students that the word "ignited" is used in the section of *In My Family* titled "Earache Treatment." Tell students that "ignited" is the targeted word for this lesson.
6. Copy the sentence from the text that contains the word "ignited." Tell students that you can often learn about a word through its context.

7. Ask students to think of similar words and phrases for "ignited." Have students discuss their ideas in pairs or small groups. When students work in groups, make sure that students who are more proficient with the language are paired with those that need more assistance. Give students time to think of words or phrases that are similar to the targeted word. The students do not need to think of synonyms or definitions of the word at this point but only related words or phrases.
8. Conduct a discussion about words or phrases related to the targeted word. An example of a discussion follows.

> **TEACHER:** What are some words or phrases that are similar to "ignited"?
>
> **STUDENTS:** Set fire, catch fire, go up in flames, set a match to, burst into flames.

TEACHER: Do you notice that our targeted word is best described by phrases? Some words are best described by more than one word as in this case. Other times words can be described with one word.

9. After students have discussed similar words and phrases for the targeted word, ask students whether the targeted word can have other forms. In this case "ignited" has the forms "ignite" and "igniting." Write the forms of the targeted word on the blanks. Remind students that they can use these additional word forms when they want to use their new vocabulary word. Provide sentences for students using the different forms as in the following example.

    The city worker needed to ignite the incinerator before work each morning.

    The firebug was igniting fires throughout the city before he was stopped.

10. Tell students that they will have a better understanding of new words if they think about the situations when the new word would be used and the people who would use this word. Pair the students into groups of two and ask students to give examples of people who would use the word "ignited." Some possible answers could be firebug, gardener, city worker. Have students discuss under what circumstances each of these people would use the word. Then have students think of additional answers.

11. Tell students that the ultimate test of vocabulary knowledge is whether they can use the word in writing. Explain to students that they have been discussing the word's meanings and using the word in conversation during their small group discussions. Ask them at this point to develop a meaningful sentence using the word. Provide an example if necessary such as the following one.

    After raking dead plants from his plot, the gardener ignited the brush and watched it burn.

12. Use Word Storm for a select group of words that you want students to learn, remember, and use in their writing. You may need to demonstrate the strategy several times before students can use it independently. Your goal, however, is to give students a short list of words, the reproducibles, and time to learn the targeted words.

NAME _____ DATE _____

WORD STORM

TARGETED WORD

_____

Sentence from the text _____

_____

_____

Similar words or phrases _____   _____

_____   _____   _____

Other forms _____   _____

People who would use this word _____

_____   _____

Sentence using the word _____

_____

NOMBRE _____ FECHA _____

WORD STORM

PALABRA

_____

Oración del texto _____

_____

_____

Palabras o frases similares _____   _____

_____   _____   _____

Otras formas _____   _____

Personas que utilizarían esta palabra _____

_____   _____

Oración utilizando esta palabra _____

_____

Recommended Children's Literature

Ada, A. F. (1997). *Gathering the sun: An alphabet in Spanish and English.* New York: HarperCollins.

Anzaldua, G. (1993). *Friends from the other side: Amigos del otro lado.* San Francisco: Children's Book Press.

Argueta, J. (2001). *A movie in my pillow: Una película en mi almohada.* San Francisco: Children's Book Press.

Blanco, A. (1994). *Angel's kite: La estrella de angel.* San Francisco: Children's Book Press.

Buchman, K. (1991). *This house is made of mud: Esta casa está hecha de lodo.* Flagstaff, AZ: Rising Moon.

Cannon, J. (1993a). *Stellaluna.* Barcelona: Editorial Juventud.

Cannon, J. (1993b). *Stellaluna.* New York: Scholastic.

Castañeda, O. S. (1993a). *Abuela's weave.* New York: Lee & Low.

Castañeda, O. S. (1993b). *El tapiz de abuela.* New York: Lee & Low Books.

Cronin, D. (2000). *Click, clack, moo: Cows that type.* New York: Simon & Schuster.

Cronin, D. (2002). *Clic, clac, muu: Vacas escritoras.* New York: Lectorum Publications.

Dominguez, K. K. (2002). *The perfect piñata: La piñata perfecta.* Morton Grove, IL: Whitman.

Dorling Kindersley. (1991). *Dinosaurs.* London: Author.

Editorial Sigmar. (1993). *Dinosaurios.* Buenos Aires, Argentina: Author.

Garza, C. L. (1996). *In my family: En mi familia.* San Francisco: Children's Book Press.

Herrera, J. F. (2002). *Grandma and me at the flea: Los meros meros remateros.* San Francisco: Children's Book Press.

Hoose, P., & Hoose, H. (1998a). *Hey, little ant.* New York: Scholastic.

Hoose, P., & Hoose, H. (1998b). *Oye, hormiguita.* New York: Scholastic.

Joose, B. M. (1991a). *Mama, do you love me?* San Francisco: Chronicle Books.

Joose, B. M. (1991b). *¿Me quieres, mamá?* San Francisco: Chronicle Books.

Levy, J. (1995). *The spirit of tío Fernando: El espiritu de tío Fernando.* Morton Grove, IL: Albert Whitman & Company.

Lowell, S. (1992a). *Los tres pequeños jabalíes.* Flagstaff, AZ: Northland.

Lowell, S. (1992b). *The three little javalinas.* Flagstaff, AZ: Northland.

Lowry, L. (1993a). *El dador.* León, Spain: Everest.

Lowry, L. (1993b). *The giver.* New York: Random House.

Mills, D., & Crouth, J. (2003). *El diente flojo, flojito, flojote: The wibbly wobbly tooth.* London: Mantra.

Orozco, J-L. (1997). *Diez deditos: Ten little fingers.* New York: Puffin.

Penn, A. (1993a). *The kissing hand.* Washington, DC: Child & Family Press.

Penn, A. (1993b). *Un beso en mi mano.* New York: Scholastic.

Pérez, A. I. (2002). *My diary from here to there: Mi diario de aquí hasta allá.* San Francisco: Children's Book Press.

Rohmer, H. (1989a). *Brother Anansi and the cattle ranch: El hermano Anansi y el rancho de ganado.* San Francisco: Children's Book Press.

Rohmer, H. (1989b). *Uncle Nacho's hat: El sombrero del tío Nacho.* San Francisco: Children's Book Press.

Veciana-Suarea, A. (2002). *Flight to freedom.* New York: Orchard.

Wood, A. (1984). *The napping house.* San Diego: Harcourt.

Wood, A. (1985). *La casa adormecida.* San Diego: Libros Viajeros.

Zubizaarreta, R., Rohmer, H., & Schecter, D. (1991). *The woman who outshone the sun: The legend of Lucia Zenteno.* San Francisco: Children's Book Press.

References

Ada, A. F. (2003). *A magical encounter: Latino children's literature in the classroom* (2nd ed.). Boston: Allyn and Bacon.

Altwerger, B., & Ivener, B. L. (1994). Self esteem: Access to literacy in multicultural and multilingual classrooms. In K. Spangengerg-Urbschat & R. Pritchard (Eds.), *Kids come in all languages: Reading instruction for ESL students*. Washington, DC: International Reading Association.

Ariza, E. N., Morales-Jones, C. A., Yahya, N., & Zainuddin, H. (2002). *Why TESOL? Theories and issues in teaching English as a second language for K–12 teachers* (2nd ed.). Dubuque, IA: Kendall/Hunt.

Baker, C. (2001). *Foundations of bilingualism and bilingual education* (3rd ed.). Buffalo, NY: Multilingual Matters.

Baumann, J. F., Kame'enui, E. F., & Ash, G. E. (2003). Research on vocabulary instruction: Voltaire redux. In J. Flood, D. Lapp, J. R. Squire, & J. M. Jensen (Eds.), *Handbook of research on teaching the English language arts* (2nd ed.) (pp. 752–785). Mahwah, NJ: Erlbaum.

Bean, T. W., & Moni, K. (2003). Developing students' critical literacy: Exploring identity construction in young adult fiction. *Journal of Adolescent & Adult Literacy, 46,* 638–648.

Bear, D. R., Templeton, S., Helman, L. A., & Baren, T. (2003). Orthographic development and learning to read in different languages. In G. G. Garcia (Ed.), *English learners: Reaching the highest level of English literacy* (pp. 71–95). Newark, DE: International Reading Association.

Beck, I. L., McKeown, M. G., Hamilton, R. L., & Kucan, L. (1997). *Questioning the author: An approach for enhancing student engagement with text.* Newark, DE: International Reading Association.

Beck, I. L., McKeown, M. G., & Kucan, L. (2002). *Bringing words to life: Robust vocabulary instruction.* New York: Guilford.

Birch, B. M. (2002). *English L2 reading: Getting to the bottom.* Mahwah, NJ: Erlbaum.

Blachowicz, C. L. Z. (1986). Making connections: Alternative to the vocabulary notebook. *Journal of Reading, 29,* 643–649.

Bourdieu, P., & Passeron, J. D. (1977). *Reproduction in education, society and culture.* Los Angeles: Sage.

Brechtel, T. (1992). *Bringing the whole together: An integrated whole-language approach for the multilingual classroom.* San Diego: Dominic.

Brisk, M. E., & Harrington, M. M. (2000). *Literacy and bilingualism: A handbook for ALL teachers.* Mahwah, NJ: Erlbaum.

Buehl, D. (2001). *Classroom strategies for interactive learning* (2nd ed.). Newark, DE: International Reading Association.

Cobb, J. (2003). *An image-based investigation into children's understandings of metacomprehension strategies: What do good readers do?* Paper presented at the National Reading Conference, Scottsdale, AZ.

Colombi, M. C., & Roca, A. (2003). Insights from research and practice in Spanish as a heritage language. In A. Roca & M. C. Colombi (Eds.), *Mi Lengua: Spanish as a heritage language in the United States* (pp. 1–21). Washington, DC: Georgetown.

Comber, B. (2001). Classroom explorations in critical literacy. In H. Fehring & P. Green (Eds.), *Critical literacy: A collection of articles from the Australian Literacy Educators' Association* (pp. 90–102). Newark, DE and South

Australia, Australia: International Reading Association and Australian Literacy Educators' Association.

Cummins, J. (2001). *Negotiating identities: Education for empowerment in a diverse society* (2nd ed.). Ontario, CA: California Association for Bilingual Education.

deBono, E. (1976). *Teaching thinking.* New York: Penguin.

Dyson, A. H. (2003). Popular literacies and the "all" children: Rethinking literacy development for contemporary childhoods. *Language Arts, 81,* 100–109.

Echevarria, J., & Graves, A. (2003). *Sheltered content instruction: Teaching English-langauge learners with diverse abilities* (2nd ed.). New York: Allyn and Bacon.

Ediger, A. (2001). Teaching children literacy skills in a second language. In M. Celce-Murcia (Ed.), *Teaching English as a second or foreign language* (3rd ed.) (pp. 153–169). Boston: Heinle & Heinle.

Escamilla, K. (2002). Bilingual means two: Assessment issues, early literacy and Spanish-speaking children. Proceedings from the Research Symposium on High Standards in Reading for students from diverse language groups: Research, Practice & Policy (pp. 100–128). Washington, DC: Office of Bilingual Education and Minority Affairs.

Fehring, H., & Green, P. (Eds.). (2001). *Critical literacy: A collection of articles from the Australian Literacy Educators' Association.* Newark, DE, and South Australia, Australia: International Reading Association and Australian Literacy Educators' Association.

Freire, P. (1985). *The politics of education: Culture, power, and liberation.* New York: Bergin & Garvey.

García, G. E. (2003). The reading comprehension development and instruction of English-language learners. In A. P. Sweet and C. E. Snow (Eds.), *Rethinking reading comprehension* (pp. 30–50). New York: Guilford.

García, G. G., & Beltrán, D. (2003). Revisioning the blueprint: Building for the academic success of English learners. In G. G. García (Ed.), *English learners: Reaching the highest level of English literacy* (pp. 197–226). Newark, DE: International Reading Association.

Gass, S. M., & Selinker, L. (2001). *Second language acquisition* (2nd ed.). Mahwah, NJ: Erlbaum.

Gee, J. P. (1996). *Social linguistics and literacies: Ideology in discourses* (2nd ed.). London: Taylor & Francis.

Gertsten, R., & Jiménez, R. (1994). A delicate balance: Enhancing literature instruction for students of English as a second language. *The Reading Teacher, 47,* 438–449.

Gillet, J., & Kita, M. J. (1979). Words, kids, and categories. *The Reading Teacher, 32,* 538–546.

Goodman, K. S. (1965). A linguistic study of cues and miscues in reading. *Elementary English, 42,* 639–643.

Green, P. (2001). Critical literacy revisited. In H. Fehring & P. Green (Eds.), *Critical literacy: A collection of articles from the Australian Literacy Educators' Association* (pp. 7–14). Newark, DE, and South Australia, Australia: International Reading Association and Australian Literacy Educators' Association.

Grongnet, A., Jameson, J., Franco, L., & Derrick-Mescua, M. (2000). *Enhancing English language learning in elementary classrooms: A training manual.* McHenry, IL: CAL & Delta Systems.

Hadaway, N. L., Vardell, S. M., & Young, T. A. (2002). *Literature-based instruction with English language learners.* Boston: Allyn and Bacon.

Hartman, D. K. (1995). Eight readers reading: The intertextual links of proficient readers reading multiple passages. *Reading Research Quarterly, 30*(3), 520–561.

Haver, J. J. (2003). *Structured English immersion: A step-by-step guide for K–6 teachers and administrators.* Thousand Oaks, CA: Corwin.

Hemmrich, H., Lim, W., & Neel, K. (1994). *Primetime!* Portsmouth, NH: Heinemann.

Herber, H. L. (1978). *Teaching reading in content areas* (2nd ed.). Englewood Cliffs, NJ: Prentice-Hall.

Hernández, A. (2003). Making content instruction accessible for English language learners. In G. G. García (Ed.), *English learners: Reading the highest level of English literacy* (pp. 125–149). Newark, DE: International Reading Association.

Hurley, S. R., & Tinajero, J. V. (2001). *Literacy assessment of second language learners.* Boston: Allyn and Bacon.

International Reading Association. (2001). *Second-language literacy instruction: A position statement of the International Reading Association.* Newark, DE: Author.

Jiménez, R. T. (2001). "It's a difference that changes us": An alternative view of the language and literacy learning needs of Latina/o students. *The Reading Teacher, 54,* 736–742.

Jiménez, R.T. (1997). The strategic reading abilities and potential for five low-literacy Latina/o readers in middle school. *Reading Research Quarterly, 32,* 224–243.

Johns, J. L., & Lenski, S. D. (2001). *Improving reading: Strategies and resources* (3rd ed.). Dubuque, IA: Kendall/Hunt.

Johns, J. L., Lenski, S. D., & Berglund, R. L. (2003). *Comprehension and vocabulary strategies for the primary grades.* Dubuque, IA: Kendall/Hunt.

Kempe, A. (2001). No single meaning: Empowering students to construct socially critical readings of the text. In H. Fehring & P. Green (Eds.), *Critical literacy* (pp. 40–57). Newark, DE and South Australia, Australia: International Reading Association and Australian Literacy Educators' Association.

Klemp, R. M. (1994). Word storm: Connecting vocabulary to the student's database. *The Reading Teacher, 48,* 282.

Kong, A., & Pearson, P. D. (2003). The road to participation: The construction of a literacy practice in a learning community of linguistically diverse learners. *Research in the Teaching of English, 38,* 85–124.

Kottler, E., & Kottler, J. A. (2002). *Children with limited English: Teaching strategies for the regular classroom* (2nd ed.). Thousand Oaks, CA: Corwin.

Lenski, S. D. (2001). Brain surfing: A strategy for making cross-curricular connections. *Reading Horizons, 42,* 21–37.

Lenski, S. D., & Johns, J. L. (2004). *Improving writing: Strategies, assessments, resources* (2nd ed.). Dubuque, IA: Kendall/Hunt.

Lenski, S. D., Wham, M. A., & Johns, J. L. (2003). *Reading & learning strategies: Middle grades through high school.* Dubuque, IA: Kendall/Hunt.

Luke, A., O'Brien, J., & Comber, B. (2001). Making community texts objects of study. In H. Fehring & P. Green (Eds.), *Critical literacy: A collection of articles from the Australian Literacy Educators' Association* (pp. 112–123). Newark, DE and South Australia, Australia: International Reading Association and Australian Literacy Educators' Association.

Lynch, A. (2003). Toward a theory of heritage language acquisition: Spanish in the United States. In A. Roca & M. C. Colombi (Eds.), *Mi Lengua: Spanish as a heritage language in the United States* (pp. 25–50). Washington, DC: Georgetown University.

Mackey, M. (1997). Good-enough reading: Momentum and accuracy in the reading of complex fiction. *Research in the Teaching of English, 31,* 428–458.

Martínez-Roldán, C. M. (2003). Building worlds and identities: A case study of the role of narratives in bilingual literature discussion. *Research in the Teaching of English, 37,* 491–526.

May, F. B. (1990). *Reading as communication* (3rd ed.). Columbus, OH: Merrill.

McLaughlin, M., & Allen, M. B. (2002). *Guided comprehension: A teaching model for grades 3–8.* Newark, DE: International Reading Association.

Meeks, L. L., & Austin, C. J. (2003). *Literacy in the secondary English classroom: Strategies for teaching the way kids learn.* Boston: Allyn and Bacon.

Meier, T. (2003). "Why can't she remember that?" The importance of storybook reading in multilingual, multicultural classrooms. *The Reading Teacher, 57,* 242–252.

Meyer, B. J. F., Brandt, K. M., & Bluth, G. J. (1980). Use of top-level structure in text: Key for reading comprehension of ninth grade students. *Reading Research Quarterly, 16,* 72–103.

Moore, D. W., & Moore, S. A. (1992). Possible sentences: An update. In E. K. Dishner, T. W. Bean, J. E. Readence, & D. W. Moore (Eds.), *Reading in the content areas* (3rd ed.) (pp. 196–202). Dubuque, IA: Kendall/Hunt.

National Center for Educational Statistics, U.S. Department of Health, Education, and Welfare. (2001). *Digest of educational statistics.* Washington, DC: U.S. Government Printing Office.

Ogle, D. M. (1986). K-W-L: A teaching model that develops active reading of expository text. *The Reading Teacher, 39,* 564–570.

Ollmann, H. E. (1991/1992). Creating higher level thinking with reading response. *Journal of Adolescent & Adult Literacy, 39,* 576–581.

Paris, S., & Jacobs, J. (1984). The benefits of informed instruction for children's reading awareness and comprehension skills. *Child Development, 55,* 2083–2093.

Peregoy, S. F., & Boyle, O. F. (2001). *Reading, writing, & learning in ESL: A resource book for K–12 teachers* (3rd ed.). New York: Addison Wesley Longman.

Pressley, M. (1995). More about the development of self-regulation: Complex, long-term, and thoroughly social. *Educational Psychologist, 30,* 207–212.

RAND Reading Study Group. (2002). *Reading for understanding: Toward an R&D program in reading comprehension.* Santa Monica, CA: Author.

Raphael, T. (1986). Teaching question-answer relationships, revisited. *The Reading Teacher, 39,* 516–522.

Rosenblatt, L. M. (1978). *The reader, the text, the poem.* Carbondale, IL: Southern Illinois University.

Rummelhart, D. E. (1980). Schemata: The building blocks of cognition. In R. J. Spiro, B. C. Bruce, & W. F. Brewer (Eds.), *Theoretical issues in reading comprehension* (pp. 33–58). Hillsdale, NJ: Erlbaum.

Schneider, J. J., & Jackson, S. A. W. (2000). Process drama: A special space and place for writing. *The Reading Teacher, 54,* 38-51.

Short, K. G., Harste, J. C., & Burke, C. (1996). *Creating classrooms for authors and inquirers* (2nd ed.). Portsmouth, NH: Heinemann.

Smith, M., & Qi, D. S. (2003). A complex tangle: Teaching writing to English language learners in the mainstream classroom. In S. Peterson (Ed.), *Untangling some knots in K–8 writing instruction* (pp. 52–65). Newark, DE: International Reading Association.

Soltero, S. W. (2004). *Dual language: Teaching and learning in two languages.* Boston: Allyn and Bacon.

Soter, A. O. (1999). *Young adult literature & the new literary theories: Developing critical readers in middle school.* New York: Teachers College Press.

Stein, N. L., & Glenn, C. G. (1979). An analysis of story comprehension in elementary school children. In R. O. Freedle (Ed.), New directions in discourse processing (pp. 53–120). Norwood, NJ: Ablex.

Teachers of English to Speakers of Other Languages (TESOL). (1997). *ESL standards for PreK–12 students.* Alexandria, VA: Author.

Vacca, R. T., & Vacca, J. L. (2003). *Content area reading: Literacy learning across the curriculum.* Boston: Allyn and Bacon.

Valdéz, G. (1998). The world outside and inside schools: Language and immigrant children. *Educational Researcher, 27,* 4–18.

Wink, J. (2001). *Critical pedagogy: Notes from the real world* (2nd ed.). New York: Longman.

Yopp, R. H., & Yopp, H. K. (2000). Sharing informational text with young children. *The Reading Teacher, 53,* 410–419.

Index

171